The Story of Medicine at Wake Forest University

Coy Cornelius Carpenter
Vice President for Medical Affairs Emeritus
Wake Forest University

THE STORY OF MEDICINE AT WAKE FOREST UNIVERSITY

by Coy C. Carpenter, M.D.

PROFESSOR OF PATHOLOGY, 1926–1970
DEAN OF THE MEDICAL SCHOOL, 1936–1963
VICE PRESIDENT FOR MEDICAL AFFAIRS, 1963–1967
VICE PRESIDENT EMERITUS, 1967–

The University of North Carolina Press
Chapel Hill

Manufactured in the United States of America
ISBN 0-8078-1150-5
Library of Congress Catalog Card Number 72-123104

TO DOROTHY
whose inspiration and partnership
kept me trying harder
and
to our "adopted daughter"
ANNE CANNON REYNOLDS FORSYTH
whose friendship, loyalty, and support
made the publication of this book possible.

Table of Contents

Introduction ix

1. *A History of the Founding of the Wake Forest College School of Medicine* 1

2. *The Two-Year School* 13

3. *The Four-Year School* 29

4. *Organization of the Medical Center* 57

5. *Wake Forest College Moves to Winston-Salem* 67

Introduction

The history of medical education at Wake Forest University is an extremely personal matter for me. The medical school had been in existence for sixty-five years when I retired on July 1, 1967, as vice president for medical affairs of the university. I had been intimately associated with the school for forty-seven of those years, as student, professor, and dean. This book is my effort to give the facts of history as I saw them. I must apologize for using the first person singular in so many places, but it is necessary in order to relate my involvement. I trust that at some future date somebody else will carry the story forward where I rest mine.

There is usually a definite place to begin the history of an institution. If the institution continues to grow and become more vital, there is seldom a place to end. Facts to be included or omitted obviously vary with the individual doing the job, and many details must be omitted to prevent the story from becoming too voluminous. This is especially true when we think of a medical school whose annual budget has increased from $20,000 to over $8 million during the past thirty years.

The medical school has been given three names since its founding in 1902. During my student days and for some time after I returned in 1926 as professor of pathology, it was known as the Wake Forest College School of Medicine. Like others in the state, it was a two-year medical school.

In 1930, a year after I became dean and two years after the school was inspected by Dr. Herman Weiskotten from the American Medical Association's Council of Medical Education, we changed the name to the Wake Forest College School of Medical Sciences to identify properly what we were trying to do at Wake Forest.

In 1941 the school was moved to Winston-Salem and became a four-year medical school associated with North Carolina Baptist Hospital. At that time it was renamed the Bowman Gray School of Medicine in honor of the late Bowman Gray, chairman of the board of R. J. Reynolds Tobacco Company, whose will provided the first money for the school's expansion.

It is difficult for me to spot the beginning of my interest in the Wake Forest medical school. I cannot remember any time in my life that I seriously thought of doing anything except study medicine at Wake Forest. Both of my brothers attended the college. Dr. L. L. Carpenter, who spent much of his life in theological education at Yale, Furman, and Baylor in addition to preaching and editing the *Biblical Recorder* (official journal of the North Carolina Baptist State Convention), graduated in 1913. Mr. C. J. Carpenter, an attorney, was graduated the following year. When my brothers first entered Wake Forest, I was a lad about ten years of age. Thumbing through the college annuals they brought home, I would pick out the medical students and study their pictures admiringly for hours.

My first real contact with Wake Forest came in the spring of 1919 when I entered as a freshman. I immediately began to worshipfully admire Dr. Thurman D. Kitchin, who had just been appointed dean of the school of medicine. Dr. Kitchin virtually took me under his arm from the time I was a freshman, and as a student many were the hours that I spent studying this man and his great philosophy and wisdom.

It was always an exciting time when the second-year students in the two-year school at Wake Forest began to think about and negotiate the transfer to a full four-year medical school. I left Wake Forest in the spring of 1922, having been accepted for my last two years at Tulane, the Medical College of Virginia, and Jefferson Medical College. During the summer I had not decided which I would accept. In late August I had a telephone call from Dr. Kitchin who told me that I had won the Harold E. Porter Scholarship to Syracuse University. Mr. Porter was a short-story writer under the pen name of Holworthy Hall. His wife was the daughter of Dean Heffron of Syracuse University College of Medicine. I knew very little about

Syracuse University at the time, but, as I have often told friends since, I would have gone to any school anywhere for a scholarship I needed very badly.

The irony of the situation is that I never received one dollar of the scholarship money. The donor went bankrupt about that time and was never able to pay the $600 a year scholarship money, but I got more at Syracuse than a scholarship. I induced a coed, Miss Dorothy Mitten, to be my wife, and she has been my inspiration and "Rock of Gibraltar" since that time.

In 1924 I was awarded the highest prize to be earned by a graduate of the Syracuse College of Medicine, appointment as assistant to the dean for the following year. The appointment included an instructorship in the Department of Pathology, headed by Dr. Herman Weiskotten. Following the year with Dr. Weiskotten, I was appointed chief resident in medicine. During the year I made plans to get a good training in internal medicine and return to North Carolina to practice.

Then I received a telegram from President William Louis Poteat of Wake Forest College, asking whether I would consider becoming professor of pathology at Wake Forest after I completed my residency. This telegram was followed later by a long letter from Dr. Kitchin. It seemed so preposterous to consider myself a professor of pathology that I circulated the telegram among my friends, making sport of the fact that I had received it. But when I showed the telegram to Dr. Weiskotten, his face became very serious and he said, "They ask whether you will consider it. You will do that, won't you?" "Do you really mean it?" I asked. Dr. Weiskotten replied that he did in all seriousness mean it and that he thought it might be a good opportunity to make a contribution to the advancement of medicine.

Two other factors induced me to accept the offer. I had planned eventually to practice medicine in North Carolina, and I considered this an opportunity to take one year of teaching while I looked for a place to practice. The other factor was that I wanted to get married and had no money. Miss Mitten and I decided that with a salary of $3,500 a year we could afford to get married, so I went to Wake Forest in the fall of 1926 as professor of pathology and one month later took unto myself a bride. Incidentally, the first year we saved $2,400 of my salary and paid on debts of education.

In consideration of a faculty for the medical school, Dr. Kitchin believed that the person who had graduated with the degree of Doctor of Medicine had learned enough about any subject to give a good course in a medical school. He believed that the type of individual the proposed faculty member might be was more important than scientific training. That thinking was, no doubt, partly the result of the discord that had prevailed in the faculty for many years. So when I went to Wake Forest in the fall of 1926 I was the only member of the medical faculty who had any graduate training in the subject which he was to teach. Today such a philosophy is unthinkable because there is so much to be known in the science of medicine and so many long years are required to become proficient enough to teach in a medical school.

When I returned to Wake Forest I discovered that great turmoil existed among the faculty, both at the medical school and in other parts of the college. At that time I did not know the subject of the controversy, and I later learned that it involved several different matters. There had been conflict within the medical school faculty for many years. Dr. Kitchin used to say, "Where there are two doctors, there are two factions." I do not think we can say that about jealousies in the practice of medicine today.

Another controversy was between Dr. William Louis Poteat, the president of Wake Forest, and the Baptists of North Carolina and concerned the teaching of the theory of evolution. I hasten to say that this was not a local controversy. It was going on throughout the state and other portions of the nation and eventually included the famous Scopes Trial in Tennessee. That particular controversy did not end until after Dr. Poteat's retirement as president. I say that particular controversy because Baptists, by tradition, have many types of controversies, the present one being concerned with the acceptance of government funds for support of their colleges and universities.

This history began to be compiled eighteen years ago when I wrote an article entitled "Wake Forest College in the Field of Medical Education, 1930–1950, and the Development of the Bowman Gray School of Medicine in Winston-Salem." I next enlisted the help of Dr. Wingate M. Johnson, who was a Winston-Salem physician and a member of the Bowman Gray faculty for many years before his death on September 11, 1963. Dr. Johnson and I collaborated and issued another unpublished history which took the school up to 1958. In 1958 the school took a great surge forward, both in academic life and expansion, and it occurred to us that we should include these developments.

The relocation of Wake Forest University and the Bowman Gray School of Medicine, and the resulting transformation within the schools, has been worth the pain and toil of all its laborers. In 1970, with the brilliant young James Ralph Scales as president of the University and the equally brilliant young Manson Meads as dean of the medical school and vice president for medical affairs, the future looks very bright indeed.

The secretarial and research staff has been willing and indispensable in getting this job done. First, there was Miss Katherine Davis. Miss Davis came to work in the school as the secretary in the Department of Anatomy. Later she became my personal secretary, and presently she serves as administrative assistant for all areas of administration. She not only has an intimate knowledge of files, places and events, she has an encyclopedic mind in remembering important facts about the school.

Miss Davis and I have been assisted by Mrs. Jerry Eller and Miss Helen Hamrick. Mrs. Katherine Johnson Jackson, daughter of Dr. Wingate Johnson, was a great help and typed one revision of our work. Elizabeth Jones Brantley has served as the guardian of my mistakes in editing and arrangement. Mrs. Brantley, now a member of the News Bureau staff at Wake Forest, has worked for several newspapers, published stories in several magazines, and served as News Bureau director at Salem College. She is the daughter of Dr. Broadus Jones, professor emeritus of English at Wake Forest, and the wife of Russell Brantley, the University's director of communications and assistant to the president.

Finally, without the work and assistance of Bill Glance, director of the Office of Information, and George Lynch, director of the Department of Audio-Visual Resources, of the Bowman Gray School of Medicine, this would never have been completed.

I am most grateful for all of this valuable help.

Three students wrote excellent papers concerning the founding of the Wake Forest College School of Medicine for their course in the history of medicine. These students were Dr. Richard Hooper, Dr. J. William Pugh, and Dr. Frank Dove. I collaborated with each of them, and they gathered information from other sources. With Dr. Hooper's permission, I am using a condensed version of the paper he wrote in 1966 for the first chapter of this book.

Coy C. Carpenter

The Story of Medicine at Wake Forest University

Entire Wake Forest College faculty, including Dr. F. K. Cooke, first dean of the medical school, and Dr. W. S. Rankin, second dean.

Chapter 1

A History of the Founding of the Wake Forest College School of Medicine

by William Richard Hooper, M.D.

An important factor in the establishment and success of the Wake Forest medical school was President C. E. Taylor's desire to see Wake Forest College expand into a college of national standing. From 1875 until his retirement as president of the college in 1905, Dr. Taylor fought debts and Baptist ministers, both of which threatened to extinguish his vision of Wake Forest's future. In his annual report to the trustees in 1894 he stated: "We are probably at a turning point in the history of the college. Before many years have passed, it will be decided whether it is to have the opportunity to expand naturally into a great institution or whether it is destined to become a small institution, whose work will be largely confined to the education of the ministry."

The outlook of the college looked worse than bleak when Dr. Taylor assumed the office of president in 1875. In the aftermath of the Civil War the never-prosperous college had been reduced to bankruptcy. An original holding of 615 acres of land had shrunk to 25, and the assets of the college stood at $15,000. Yet upon his retirement, the assets of the college amounted to $357,000. As a reporter from the Raleigh *News and Observer* said, he did "this without furor, without exploitation, in fact—inexplicably." The specter of bankruptcy may have been the lesser of two problems with which Dr. Taylor had to cope, for then as today a controversy raged over Wake Forest's role in education. Was the college to educate Baptists for the ministry, or would it assume a larger educational role? The president of the college believed that Wake Forest could do no less than become a "great institution." Dr. Taylor's genius lay in getting tasks done without controversy, and in his characteristic manner he quietly succeeded in establishing a school of law and a school of medicine.

Dr. Taylor did not let his zeal to enlarge his college's horizons blind him to the fact that any ambitious financial venture might well exhaust the shoestring resources of the institution. He believed that the college should maintain high academic standards and create leaders dedicated to improving the state and the South. His belief undoubtedly saved him from falling prey to the temptation to which many presidents of better endowed schools succumbed, that of establishing medical diploma mills as a means of adding revenue to their colleges. In his 1902 report to the trustees, Dr. Taylor explained why Wake Forest could offer successfully only two years of medical instruction: ". . . I am persuaded that, in view of existing conditions in North Carolina, you (the trustees) would act wisely in carrying out your expressed purpose of providing for two years of medical instruction. The conferring of a medical degree here has never been proposed by anyone. Only an institution which can offer the advantage of great hospitals and extensive clinical opportunities of a large city is in position to do this."

Although the original suggestion of establishing a medical department at Wake Forest was submitted on May 31, 1893, to the Board of Trustees, it was not until 1900 that Dr. Taylor wholeheartedly endorsed this proposal. The opening of a two-year medical school hinged upon the success of the newly opened law school, and it is significant that the committee selected in 1893 to inquire into the possibilities of establishing a medical school did not report until the 1896 meeting of the board. At that time Dr. Taylor reported the law school a "phenomenal success"; nevertheless, the opening of the school of medicine lay years in the future, hampered primarily by lack of funds. It seems more than coincidence that Dr. Taylor's recommendation for establishing a medical school coincided with the announcement that sufficient funds had been raised to erect the Alumni Building. The medical school was housed in this building after its completion in 1905 until the erection of the William Amos Johnson Medical Building in 1932. Professor J. B. Carlyle was instrumental not only in getting money for the Alumni Building, but during his fund raising drive he was able to secure $1,000 as an initial donation for an infirmary. The erection of an infirmary was also strongly supported by Dr. Fred K. Cooke, the first dean of the medical school, because an infirmary would enable him to offer better care to the student body. This in reality became a community hospital and led to conflict between members of the medical faculty to the extent that the management of the hospital was taken from the doctors by the trustees.

The medical department was scheduled to open in the fall of 1901, and the inauguration of the new program had even been hastily advertised on the final page of the catalogue. However, a committee appointed by the trustees failed to select a qualified dean. In his 1902 report Dr. Taylor again urged that the trustees take action on the proposal to establish a medical department, reminding them that several students had come to the college planning to study medicine and had to be turned away. Only one month before the beginning of the fall term of 1902, Dr. Fred K. Cooke, a surgeon in the U.S. Army, was selected to head the medical department.

First medical building on old campus at Wake Forest

Dr. Cooke had no outstanding qualifications for the job other than he was a graduate of Tulane Medical School, perhaps then the finest medical school in the South. He seems to have been highly recommended by E. W. Timberlake, a member of the Board of Trustees. The young physician was also the son of a member of the Board of Trustees, Judge C. M. Cooke. Nevertheless, the board's selection of Dr. Cooke was indeed fortunate because the young man was as loyal to the college as was his father and as interested in establishing a fine medical school as was Dr. Taylor.

The reasons for embarking upon a medical career were undoubtedly as numerous in 1902 as they are today. Perhaps some men were drawn to Wake Forest because of the proximity of "the capital of the State," which the 1902 catalogue boasted "affords many of the advantages, without the moral dangers of city life." Dr. Taylor reported to the trustees in 1898 that there were demands among the students planning to become missionaries that a medical department be established. At least one member of the class of 1903 reported that he had decided to begin the study of medicine when his fiancée had refused to be a farmer's bride. For whatever their reasons, thirteen medical students began their careers at Wake Forest College in the fall of 1902.

The committee that selected Dr. Cooke as dean had wisely avoided a pitfall that would have ruined the school before it began. It had been suggested, in order to save funds, that the trustees hire a Raleigh physician to oversee the students by commuting to the school on a twice weekly basis. The committee rejected the proposal because it was unsound from an educational point of view, adding that such a step would require the hiring of an assistant and the school would actually save little money.

Growth and Accreditation

The new dean shared Dr. Taylor's view that the medical instruction must be of high quality, and he was determined that the department be well equipped and supplied with a large number of pathologic specimens. In a note prefaced by the news that the medical school had cost less than expected, Dr. Taylor asked the trustees for additional funds to complete the equipping of the laboratories. Dr. Cooke also felt that the department needed another professor, and his opinion must have been shared by Dr. Taylor because the 1902–3 catalogue lists a vacant chair of histology, embryology, materia medica, and therapeutics. Although the catalogue assured the reader that this chair would be filled the next year, no mention in the minutes of the Board of Trustees is made of "hiring" a second man for the medical school until May, 1903. Yet, the trustees acquiesced to the dean's wishes even though it meant scraping up an additional $1250 for salary per annum.

When Dr. Randolph Winslow, professor of surgery at the University of Maryland, came to Wake Forest to inspect the facilities of the new school for the American Medical Association, Dr. Cooke inquired about a suitable man to fill the vacant chair in his department and was advised to write Dr. William Welch at Johns Hopkins. Dr. Welch was not only one of the most eminent pathologists in the world, he was also vitally interested in improving the quality of American medical education. By recommending Dr. Watson S. Rankin for the chair, he assured Dr. Cooke not only of a competent pathologist but of a man as interested as the dean in establishing a good school. Dr. Taylor had suggested in his 1903 report to the trustees that only a part-time assistant be hired. However, Dr. Cooke was able to persuade the medical committee to appoint a full-time professor.

His determination to set high standards for the medical school brought him in conflict with some members of the faculty as well as with some of his own students. In his May 19, 1904 report to the trustees, Dr. Cooke denied charges that the medical department had been a financial burden upon the school and reminded the trustees that the laboratories of histology, bacteriology, and pathology were the best equipped in the state. In this same report Dr. Cooke said that three of the six students who had passed their first year's work had left the school to take their second year elsewhere. Dr. Cooke had enclosed in his report a letter written by the students explaining their action. Even though this letter is now lost, the fact that seven of the thirteen students had not passed their work and that three of the six who had passed preferred to take their training elsewhere makes it seem likely that the letter contained protests charging that their dean was "tough as nails." However, the controversy was perhaps not as serious as Dr. Cooke imagined. His gastric ulcer left him continually in pain; his zeal led him to believe that his ulcers hampered him from carrying out his duties efficiently; his fear of doing an inadequate job made the dean overly sensitive to any criticism.

Dr. Cooke's determination to make his school second to none was rewarded when the young school was accepted into membership of the Association of American Medical Colleges in 1904. The only other school in the state which heretofore had been received into membership was the University of North Carolina's two-year school at Chapel Hill. In 1904 and in prior years a half dozen or more other "unapproved" medical schools existed in North Carolina.

His ulcer forced Dr. Cooke to retire suddenly at the end of the 1905 school year, and he died a year later from complications of the disorder. The rapidity with which the school was accepted into membership in the Association of American Colleges is a monument to a young man who pursued his goal tirelessly in the face of an intractable illness.

Dr. Rankin, who succeeded Dr. Cooke as dean, had taken two years at the University of North Carolina before completing his education at the University of Maryland Medical School. His ability was demonstrated in 1901 by a year's residence at Johns Hopkins, as well as by his pioneer work in the eradication of hookworm disease in the South. Dr. Rankin came to Wake Forest "to put the school on the map." Impressed by Welch and Osler's desire to improve the quality of American medical education, the young man gave up his practice in Onslow County to take a low-paying position at Wake Forest, convinced that this was a golden opportunity to make a significant contribution to his profession. His first task was to find a man to occupy the chairs of anatomy and physiology which Dr. Cooke had vacated. Dr. Lewis M. Gaines of Atlanta had high qualifications, being a graduate of Hampden-Sydney College in 1898 with the B.A. and B.S. degrees. After a year of graduate study at the University of Virginia, he went to Johns Hopkins where he received his degree of Doctor of Medicine in 1903. Before beginning his surgical practice in Atlanta, Dr. Gaines had been the assistant surgeon in the Rhode Island Hospital, and on his examination by the North Carolina Board of Medical Examiners in 1905, Dr. Gaines stood highest among 137 applicants. Perhaps it was partially in fear of being overshadowed by his well-trained "assistant" that Dr. Rankin took special summer courses at Harvard in 1906.

The two men made a good team to expand the facilities of their small school. Their energy was that of inexhaustible youth, their ideas those which older men would not dare dream, and for a time it seemed that without money and in a village with a population of 814 they would build a great medical center. In 1907 they announced to the *News and Observer* their intention of opening a pathology clinic to which physicians could send biopsies for diagnosis.

The newly opened infirmary afforded Dr. Gaines the opportunity of starting his own little North Carolina Baptist Hospital. By means of the *Biblical Recorder* on July 31, 1907, he invited all Baptists who could not undertake a long and expensive journey to a great city for treatment to come to Wake Forest. "Reclining on (the hospital's) porches, surrounded by trees and flowers, lulled to rest by varied songs of the birds so numerous in this particular spot, invalids could not fail to drink in health and vigor with every breath of pure country air."

During his stay at Wake Forest Dr. Rankin wrote additional articles on the prevalence of hookworm among the student body, demonstrating that the disease had a much higher incidence in North Carolina than was generally suspected. His work led to the eradication of the disease in the southern United States by calling the attention of the Rockefeller Foundation to its prevalence, and the reputation of the young medical school was enhanced by this research.

In spite of all this activity, Dr. Rankin's primary interest was that of training good physicians. The late Dr. Wingate Johnson recounted an incident showing that the dean felt that physicians should have high moral standards as well as be competent in the medical sciences.

> In the fall of 1904, Dr. Rankin initiated the honor system in the medical classes which he taught, many years before it was established for the whole student body. After writing the questions for his first quiz on the blackboard, he walked out of the classroom, leaving the students without supervision. Unfortunately, one member of the class was unscrupulous enough to refer to his notes during the examination. A self-appointed committee of three students then went to Dr. Rankin and, without revealing the culprit's name, asked that Dr. Rankin stay in the room when the next quiz was given. Instead of doing so, however, he delivered a blistering denunciation of any prospective doctor whose moral integrity could not be trusted. So far as is known, the offense was never repeated.

Dr. Rankin's philosophy of medical education was simple: there were too many unqualified doctors in the United States, and the only basis for the existence of the Wake Forest medical school was to train good physicians. It seemed unlikely that a school boasting a mere two professors and thirty-five students could have national attention focused upon it, but because of Dr. Rankin's demand that Wake Forest be known for the quality of the student it graduated, the *Journal of the American Medical Association* listed the Wake Forest medical school

First anatomy dissecting room in basement of gymnasium

as one of eleven that required two years of college work for entrance in its 1908 report on United States medical schools.

The admission requirements had gradually become more stringent, and they were designed in part to screen out the ever-growing number of applicants to the medical school. Dr. Rankin was also anxious to comply with the requirements the American Medical Association had begun to recommend for medical schools. The 1902–3 catalogue, the first that gave a complete description of the medical courses, did not segregate medical from preliminary courses, and it was not required that the medical student remain at Wake Forest until he fulfilled the requirements for a B.S. degree. Although a student would have been hard put to complete successfully the medical courses without some preliminary background, it was not until 1907–8 that Wake Forest entered the magic circle which it shared with Harvard and Johns Hopkins and eight other schools by requiring two years of premedical training. Indeed, the prospective medical student who was trying to decide upon a school might have even been persuaded by the Wake Forest catalogue that the college's medical program offered advantages over its larger northern counterparts:

It is generally recognized that the eight years of collegiate work required for the baccalaureate and medical degree is frequently too severe a tax on the nervous and financial capital of deserving students; and of late years many remedies have been suggested. The suggestion which has received the strongest support and which this department adopts is to combine the academic and medical training in such a way as to preserve the advantages of each, and at the same time make it possible for the student to graduate with the baccalaureate degree and the medical degree in six years.

Dean Rankin reported to the trustees that the medical school had membership in both the Association of American Medical Colleges and the New York Board of Regents, an honor shared with only three other southern schools, all of the others being located outside the Tar Heel State.

The school was to receive additional recognition when Dr. N. P. Colwell visited Wake Forest in connection with the historic 1910 report of Abraham Flexner. Dr. Rankin recalls that the distinguished visitor arrived on a Sunday, and when he was taken to the Alumni Building, Dr. Rankin found that he did not have his key. An unlocked window afforded an unpretentious but effective entrance for Dr. Colwell. Nevertheless, he wrote that "the laboratories of this little school are, as far as they go, models in their way. Everything about them indicates intelligence and earnestness." However, the report also stated that there was no pharmacology and that physiology was "slight." The late Dr. Wingate Johnson also stated, "The physiology course in the early days of the school consisted solely of lectures, supplemented by reading the then popular Kirke's manual. What has been termed the scientific use of the imagination was required to visualize the various physcologic processes that are now demonstrated in the laboratory." This state of affairs was rectified by Dr. W. T. Carstarphen's acceptance of the chair of physiology and pharmacology in 1910.

Student Life

In many respects the life of the Wake Forest medical student differed but little from that of its Bowman Gray counterpart. The drudgery of seemingly endless anatomy labs took its toll upon medical students in 1905, just as it does today, although the elegant term "paranoid" had not become a part of medical student lingo. Dr. Johnson said: "Soon as the work of dissection began, the morals of the whole class were slightly lowered; those of us who could neither smoke nor chew began to envy those who could, and some began taking lessons on the use of the weed. The rest of us never went into the dissecting hall without our pockets full of matches, which we cheerfully furnished to anyone who would volunteer to smoke."

The routine of all medical schools in whatever age must be one of endless quizzes and practical exams, and the late Dr. Wingate Johnson, the historian of the class of 1905, could well be reporting for any class when he said "all kinds of scores (were made) on them." However, the medical student of the two-year school may have been held in slightly higher esteem by his fellow Wake Forest students than his counterpart of today because of the fraternities' demand during initiations for skulls issued to the medical students.

George Washington Paschal states in his history of Wake Forest College that the cadavers were sometimes treated with "indignity." Pranksters enjoyed hanging them from trees near the gymnasium which also doubled as the anatomy laboratory, and Paschal also notes that at night people used the "longer and less gruesome streets around the campus" in preference to the walks near the gymnasium.

Foundation for the Future

Dr. Rankin's work with the Wake Forest medical school was widely acclaimed and resulted in an offer from the state of North Carolina in 1909 to become its first full-time secretary of the Board of Health. He remained at this post until 1925 when he became the director of the hospital section of the Duke Endowment. He remained a warm friend of his adopted college, serving as a trustee of the college from 1909 until 1929. It was largely through his efforts that Dr. Thurman D. Kitchin became dean of the medical school at a critical point in its history, and in his capacity as a director of the Duke Endowment, Dr. Rankin secured funds for the enlargement of North Carolina Baptist Hospital in conjunction with the establishment of the Bowman Gray School of Medicine. His life-long efforts on behalf of Wake Forest College were recognized by the school in 1925 when he was awarded an honorary D.Sc. At this time, 1966, at the age of ninety, Dr. Rankin serves as a consultant to the Hospital and Orphan Sections of the Duke Endowment.

When the young dean resigned his position in 1909, there could be no doubt of the correctness of the position which he and Dr. Cooke had taken—that of demanding a high quality of work from the students in their charge. Their concern for high standards had brought the medical school recognition from two of the most eminent accrediting agencies in the United States. Thus, the school was so well established in 1909 that it was able to survive the years of faculty wrangling which occurred after the resignation of Dr. Rankin.

Bowman Gray

Chapter 2

The Two-Year School

The Early Years: 1909–1929

Between 1909, when Dr. Rankin resigned the deanship, and 1929, the medical school operated as a school of basic sciences. The teaching was largely didactic and the laboratories were poorly equipped and used largely to demonstrate fundamentals. The curriculum was the standard traditional group of courses arranged in the traditional manner.

In the early days of this period, extensive discord developed among the faculty. The office of dean was eliminated, and each faculty member assumed a portion of its responsibility.

In 1917 Dr. Thurman D. Kitchin, a general practitioner in Scotland Neck, North Carolina, was elected professor of physiology and pharmacology. Dr. Kitchin grew up in Scotland Neck and was the sixth of eight Kitchin brothers who went to Wake Forest. He was graduated in 1905, having begun to study medicine during his last year, and attended the University of North Carolina School of Medicine for one year. He received the M.D. degree from Jefferson Medical College in 1908, and in the examination for license by the North Carolina State Board of Medical Examiners he made the highest grade in his group. Before he returned to Wake Forest as a professor, he had practiced medicine for two years in Lumberton and for seven years in Scotland Neck.

Thurman D. Kitchin
Dean of Wake Forest College School of Medicine, 1919–1936
President of Wake Forest College, 1930–1950

In 1919 the office of dean was re-established, and Dr. Kitchin was elected to that position. He served until 1930 when I became dean. However, when I joined the faculty in 1926 as professor of pathology, Dr. Kitchin was in very poor health and delegated the greater portion of the responsibilities of the medical school to me.

Dr. Kitchin's Presidency

Dr. Kitchin became president of the college in 1930 and served for twenty years. For the first five years after he was made president, Dr. Kitchin retained the title of dean of the medical school as well as president of the college, but during those five years I, without portfolio, directed the affairs of the medical school. In 1935 I was appointed assistant dean, and in 1936 I was made dean.

Concrete evidence of the substantial growth of the college during Dr. Kitchin's twenty years as president is found in a comparison of its status in 1930 with that in 1950.

	1930	1950	
Enrollment	617	2160	
Faculty	46	187	
Budget	$ 300,000	$2,000,000	
Endowment	$2,300,000	$4,536,000	(Exclusive of Reynolds fund)
Physical plant	$ 681,000	$3,643,000	

Dr. Kitchin's achievements are all the more remarkable when it is remembered that he had a heart attack before he was elected president and another about two years before he left office. A final attack on August 28, 1955, proved fatal.

In 1932 the William Amos Johnson Medical Building was erected as a memorial by the family of this bright young man who taught anatomy for only a year before he was killed in an automobile accident in November 1927. The school moved from its cramped quarters in the Alumni Building. The student body in the medical school was slightly increased, and this building provided ample space for the school at the level at which it operated until it was moved to Winston-Salem.

Move to Winston-Salem: Background

In 1929 the North Carolina Baptist State Convention met in Shelby. Dr. Kitchin and I went to the convention as messengers from the

First North Carolina Baptist Hospital Building, 1928

Wake Forest church. We discussed with several of the Baptist leaders the possibility of interesting business leaders in Winston-Salem in providing funds for moving the Wake Forest College School of Medicine to Winston-Salem. We pointed out the advantages of linking the school with the North Carolina Baptist Hospital and of having activities for ministering to the sick conducted by the Baptists united in the same location. We found general agreement with the idea, but funds to finance the move were not found.

On November 14, 1929, the following story, written by C. S. Green, was published in the Raleigh *News and Observer:*

MEDICAL SCHOOL MAY BE MOVED

Wake Forest College medical school may be moved to Winston-Salem, and co-ordinated with the Baptist Hospital in that city. This developed from conversation and unofficial conferences of alumni here today.

Egbert L. Davis, Winston-Salem, president of the Alumni Association, and on the board of the Baptist Hospital, said that an opinion seems to prevail among alumni with whom the matter was discussed that developments in the near future may lead to such a move on the part of Wake Forest College officials.

President Francis P. Gaines, and Dr. Thurman D. Kitchin, head of the medical school, would make no statement concerning the matter. It was admitted, though, by Mr. Davis and others, that the idea is not new, that it has been mentioned quietly for several years, and that the time seems ripe for a definite consideration of the proposal.

The statement given out by Mr. Davis is:

"The Wake Forest medical school is under consideration by alumni and interested citizens of Winston-Salem, and may be joined with the Baptist Hospital and training school for nurses there. This idea has gained favor rapidly with alumni who have discussed the matter.

"Many universities have their medical schools at cities away from the seat of the university. The work of Wake Forest medical school and the Baptist Hospital and the training school for nurses would produce logical and mutual co-ordination. It would remove much duplication in the work in each of these units and make the work of each more efficient.

"And at the same time relief would be given somewhat to the congestion at Wake Forest, giving more classroom and laboratory space for other departments of the college. It would enable the medical school to broaden its fields and since Winston-Salem already has ample hospital facilities, and eminent doctors which are essential things in the last two years of the medical course, Winston-Salem may in the near future have a full four-year medical school, in connection with our hospital plant, equal to any in the country."

The great world-wide economic depression started that same month and year, and by 1930 a large segment of the population of the United States was in financial distress. Many physicians could not collect in fees sufficient funds for their support, and some even turned to other lines of endeavor to earn a living.

The depression created a lack of buying power that provided an apparent surplus of many goods and services, including medical care. Cattle were destroyed to save the cost of feed, and farmers were asked to plow under every third row of cotton to reduce the supply. Some leaders in the American Medical Association decided that the supply of doctors should, likewise, be reduced.

It is interesting to note here that the Bowman Gray School of Medicine was developed because of a movement to limit the number of doctors in this country by closing the two-year medical schools. Now we recognize the shortage of doctors, and millions are being spent to expand old schools and build new ones.

The Medical School Controversy

There was some disagreement between leaders in the American Medical Association on the method of reducing the number of doctors.

Some thought that some of the smaller and weaker schools should be closed.

Aside from the matter of the supply of doctors, the pendulum in medical education had begun to swing toward more practical or hospital training, commonly used for instruction, in the fundamental sciences of anatomy, chemistry, and physiology.

In 1933 the Council on Medical Education of the American Medical Association and the Association of American Medical Colleges began a joint inspection of all medical schools with Dr. H. G. Weiskotten, dean of the College of Medicine of Syracuse University, in charge of the survey. Dr. Weiskotten spent April 15, 16, and 17, 1935, at Wake Forest. He was accompanied by Dr. Harold D. Rypins, secretary of the Board of Medical Examiners of New York State, and Mrs. Rypins.

When the inspection was completed, Dr. Weiskotten and Dr. Rypins reported to President Kitchin that the medical school would have to close. Afterwards I drove Dr. Weiskotten and Dr. and Mrs. Rypins to Durham. Since I was a former pupil and associate of Dr. Weiskotten, we discussed freely what I should do after the school was closed. That was on Saturday. After a conference with Dr. Kitchin, I made an appointment with Dr. Weiskotten for a conference in Durham the next morning. At that conference Dr. Weiskotten was adamant in his position that the school would have to close.

It was evident to Dr. Kitchin that the inspection of medical schools was a means of "justifying" the withdrawal of approval of the smaller schools, particularly the two-year schools, since they were thought to have insufficient prestige to defend themselves successfully.

Following an interview with Dr. Kitchin, the Raleigh *News and Observer* wrote on October 1, 1935, editorially, as follows.

PLOWING UP DOCTORS

If Dr. Thurman Kitchin, president of Wake Forest College, is correct in his explanation of the proposal of the Council on Medical Education of the American Medical Association to close the medical schools at Chapel Hill and Wake Forest, then the time has come to change an old injunction. "Physician, heal thyself" should be altered to "Physician, diagnose thyself." For if, as Dr. Kitchin says, organized physicians are deliberately undertaking to create a scarcity profitable to themselves in the practice of medicine, the practitioners of an ancient, an honorable, a learned profession ought to realize that they are not immune to the disease of rapaciousness which is the plague of our times.

Dr. Kitchin, in commenting on the proposal of the Council to eliminate all two-year medical schools in the country, made the deliberate and unequivocal charge that the whole purpose of the Council of the Association is to limit the number of physicians in order that competition may be reduced in the medical profession, and that professional profits may so be safeguarded. In other words, he held that the Council on Education was interested not in the standards of education of medical students, but in the financial welfare of already licensed practitioners. (Both the Chapel Hill and Wake Forest schools have the highest standards and their students take high rank in the larger schools in which they receive the last two years of their training.)

Undoubtedly a serious situation has been created in some states by what seems on the surface to be an over-supply of doctors. In some sections, indeed, the proportion of doctors is as high as one doctor among every 400 people. As a result, doctors have been unable to make a living, not to speak of a return on the large investment in dollars and time which a modern medical education means. In other sections, however, as, for instance, North Carolina, the proportion of doctors to the population is much lower, so low in some sections that doctors are desperately needed and not available.

But no matter how great or small is the proportion of doctors to patients, the spectacle of doctors unable to make a living in a land where the medical care of the people is still inadequate is one which calls for statesmanship and not the tactics of the monopolist. The doctor, who has spent many years and much money in acquiring the training essential to the practice of that profession which serves humanity, ought to be able to make a living commensurate with his training and skill. But such a living ought not to be dependent upon a reduction of the number of physicians. The trouble which plagues the physician is not a surplus of doctors but a scarcity of human use of the doctors' skill.

There is plenty of work to be done. There are plenty of human beings everywhere who need and do not have the ministrations of the trained physicians. Certainly until the last sick human has the benefit of wholly adequate medical attention there will be no surplus of doctors. In North Carolina particularly, a great rural population needs the attention of doctors. It needs doctors whose eduction, while quite as good, was secured at a lower cost—as it can be in the two-year schools at Wake Forest and Chapel Hill—and who can therefore serve for a smaller return. The people of this State are not able to pay such fees to doctors, who have paid the high costs of medical education in the larger institutions outside the State and at Duke, must charge if they are to make a fair return upon the time and money they spent in acquiring their skills.

To insist that only the more expensive type of medical education be permitted is not only to restrict the number of doctors to those able to pay the higher fees of the bigger schools, but also to increase the investment in education on which physicians hope to make a return and for which patients must pay. This program of plowing up doctors is a species of the all too prevalent monopolistic practices of organizations of crafts and professions, from plumbers and cosmetologists to doctors and lawyers, of keeping down competition for the benefit of those already in. In the case of the doctors it is probably as stupid as it is inhuman. Such practices more than anything else are hastening the approach of state medicine, which a majority of practicing physicians seem to oppose. Such practices also will result in the growth of the number of quacks who practice furtively around and under the association of the medically elite. Such practices reduce the organized medical profession from a learned society to a union for the safeguarding of profits.

Plowing up cotton was an emergency measure justified only by the crisis of the depression. But plowing up doctors, not merely for the present but for the whole future in which men who might now be educated would be denied education and admittance to the profession, would be plowing up humanity in order that profits might be reaped.

The council was soon to learn the great mistake of the assumption that smaller schools could not defend themselves. Dr. Kitchin contacted deans of other two-year medical schools, wrote letters, and issued statements to the press. At the time, there were ten two-year medical schools: Alabama, Dartmouth, University of Mississippi, Missouri, University of North Carolina, University of North Dakota, University of South Dakota, Utah, Wake Forest, and University of West Virginia. Dr. Kitchin's statement, published in the Raleigh *News and Observer* on October 2, 1935, follows.

FEWER DOCTORS?

Today's *News and Observer* quotes me as stating that the decision of the Council on Medical Education and Hospitals to close the Wake Forest College and University of North Carolina medical schools was a deliberate attempt to reduce the number of doctors in the country. I am further quoted as saying, "It is my belief that the schools to be eliminated were selected before the inspection was ever made and that the inspection was made not for the purpose of improving medical education but was deliberately made for the purpose of securing information which would justify the powers that be in eliminating the schools which had been selected as those to be eliminated." And further, "It is evident that the powers that be in American medical education decided to reduce the number of medical students." Apparently the closing of the two-year schools is the first step.

I am correctly quoted and I wish now to support these statements with direct quotations from those who control medical education; especially quoting from Dr. William D. Cutter, secretary of the Council on Medical Education, who has charge of the Survey of Medical Education. The inspector is responsible to and reports to Cutter. In everyday parlance, Cutter is the whole show and is the virtual dictator of medical education in America.

In an address before the annual meeting of the Association of American Medical Colleges, October 31, 1933, at the launching of this movement, Dr. Cutter said:

"You, who sit before me, hold in your hands the key to this situation. You, and you alone, are in a position to eliminate the excess production of doctors. Not that this can be easily achieved. Though all of you might agree with me that the number of medical graduates should be reduced, there will not be any unanimity of opinion as to which schools should do the reducing. I can imagine someone saying that the large schools should initiate the pruning, that no entering class should exceed 100; and then I can hear the report that the large schools are also the very good schools, and that the reduction should be made through the elimination of those institutions which have failed to receive substantial support."

Dr. Ray Walters in an address before the annual convention on Medical Education, Chicago, February 18, 1935, said:

"Dr. William D. Cutter suggests that 'medical education is costly not only to the individual but to society' and that 'not everyone who aspires to a professional career has the God-given right to receive a long and highly technical training at public cost.' "

Again quoting from Dr. Cutter: "The college authorities must do one of two things, either reduce the number of their students or else warn them before it is too late that the mere fact of having attended college does not guarantee them entrance into professional vocations. If higher education is going to make them dissatisfied, they had better stay away from college."

An astonishing statement from any man who is at all concerned for the higher education of our people in general or for a higher standard of professional life. It is positively ridiculous to warn a man against a college career because it may make him dissatisfied with his present status or prospects. What is education for but to inspire in him a noble discontent?

Dr. Walter B. Bierring in his presidential address before the American Medical Association in June, 1934, said:

"It is only natural to place the responsibility with the medical schools, in that they hold in their hands the power to control the supply of physicians for the future, but the time has arrived for the American Medical Association to take the initiative and point the way. During the coming year the association, through the Council on Medical Education and Hospitals, will institute a resurvey of the medical schools of this country. Whether the problems of this new day in medicine will be met by a limitation in the number of existing institutions or the number of students admitted cannot be foretold, but it will require real courage and tenacity to bend the educational processes to the urgent social and economic needs of the changing order. A fine piece of education work could well be done if we were to use only one-half of the 70-odd medical schools in the United States.

"It will be claimed that to close educational doors of any kind to ambitious youth is undemocratic and un-American; that, if a young man or woman wants to study medicine and can pass the necessary examinations, he or she should be free to do so. Yet, if I read the signs right, the truly democratic process will be to take thought about the good of the whole, and less about the special satisfaction of the few. In one of the enlightened democracies of the old world, Sweden, this is being successfully accomplished. It will also be argued that in a democracy of 48 states the control of the number of physicians to be licensed is the prerogative of the individual state. A precedent has, however, been established by our neighbor to the north in the province of Alberta, where legislation was recently adopted that no more physicians will be registered in the province until the proportion has risen to one for 1,200 of population."

The Council on Medical Education met in Denver, Colorado, in September, 1935, and voted that in the future it would not recognize any two-year medical schools. By that time presidents and deans of colleges and universities had been stimulated to activity by Dr. Kitchin. Members of the Association of American Medical Colleges began to resent the authority assumed by the council and to recognize that the college association's participation in the medical school survey was a farce. Accordingly, the Association of American Medical Colleges at its annual meeting held in Toronto, Canada in October loudly protested the high-handed action of the Council on Medical Education and voted unanimously to ask the council to rescind its action that would close all two-year schools. On December 9 the council, meeting in Chicago, voted to rescind the action, but the plight of the two-year schools was not so easily relieved. There was continued effort to expand the two-year schools at Wake Forest and Chapel Hill.

The 1937 state legislature authorized Governor Clyde R. Hoey to appoint a medical school commission to study the needs and make recommendations before the meeting of the 1939 legislature. The commission appointed by Governor Hoey was composed of the following persons: Dr. T. W. M. Long, chairman, Dr. William Coppridge, secretary, Hon. O. M. Mull, Dr. B. J. Lawrence, Joe Garrett, Dr. W. M. MacNider, and Dr. C. C. Carpenter. An attempt was made to induce Mr. Mull to take the chairmanship of the commission, but he declined, stating that in his opinion the chairman should be a doctor.

In the beginning, I made it clear that I considered the commission to be a state agency, and as such, its work should be directed toward consideration of the state university medical school. I visualized no way that a fusion could be brought about between the church related school and a state school.

Members of the commission visited other medical schools, surveyed opinion from doctors and nurses, and made a study of the entire problem. In the fall of 1938, as the time of the next General Assembly was drawing near, Mr. Mull came into a meeting and announced that a committee to select the beneficiary of a large charitable fund had expressed a willingness to make a commitment to the medical school, provided it could be located in the home city of the donor. Dr. MacNider vigorously objected to the consideration of any location for the school other than Chapel Hill. When the meeting adjourned, I approached Mr. Mull and asked him to assist in getting the fund for the Wake Forest Medical School since it was evident that there was violent objection to moving the Chapel Hill school to another location. Mr. Mull answered that he could not work for Wake Forest as a member of the commission appointed to consider the needs of the state university medical school. He promised, however, to work on behalf of Wake Forest as soon as the commission filed its report with the governor. The final report of the commission was completed that fall at a meeting in Raleigh. Mr. Mull was unable to attend but sent a statement with the request that it be attached to the report.

The report summarized was as follows.

THE COMMISSION RECOMMENDS:

1. The establishment in the state of a four-year degree granting medical school of the best grade.
2. That it be a part of the University of North Carolina.
3. That it be a part of an addition to the present plant at Chapel Hill.
4. That a 300 bed hospital is needed, to cost with accessories $1,500,000, and that $200,000 additional yearly appropriations will be necessary for its maintenance.
5. That such an institution will serve several urgent needs in the state.
6. That the institution be established as soon as is practicable.
7. That in the event it has to be deferred
   a. full support be given the present school
   b. a Commission continue to study the plan and devise ways and means for its furtherance.

Mr. Mull's statement follows.

I concur in the report of the Commission in that there is a need for a Medical School, owned and operated by the State. I therefore offered an

Honorable Odus M. Mull

amendment to the report "striking out all reference in the report to any location of the Medical School to be built." The report locates the School at Chapel Hill.

My reason for offering the amendment was that responsible parties had promised that a large donation would be made from available private funds to supplement a state appropriation to build a Medical School and to endow it, provided the School was built at a designated city in the State. That the School should be a unit of the Greater University of the state and operated by its Trustees, similar to State College at Raleigh and our College for Women at Greensboro, but must be built in the home city of the donors.

Dr. MacNider, who is Dean of the two-year School of Medicine at the University, and is a member of the Commission, stated that if the Medical School was not located at the University, it would be a failure, and that he had rather for the state to have no Medical College, unless it was located at Chapel Hill. The Amendment was defeated—four members voted against—two voted for—and one was absent.

I do not think the location of the Medical School at Chapel Hill is of sufficient importance to make it necessary to refuse a large donation which was conditioned upon building the School elsewhere.

I have discussed the State's financial situation with individual members of the "Budget Commission" and also with the Governor of the State and it is the unanimous opinion of those officials that the State acting alone, could not at this time provide sufficient funds for such a new undertaking.

I think it would be better for the state to accept a large donation from private parties and build a Medical College at the designated city in the state rather than have no Medical College. I believe the action of the Commission makes it impossible for the State to build a Medical College at this time and for that reason I cannot favor the report.

Founding of the Bowman Gray School of Medicine

The day following the completion of the report of the medical school commission, I went to Shelby and conferred with Mr. Mull and Governor Hoey. They advised me to go to Winston-Salem and quietly find out whether leaders connected with the North Carolina Baptist Hospital would co-operate in moving the medical school to Winston-Salem if financial support could be obtained through the charitable fund left in the will of the late Bowman Gray.

I spent three days in Winston-Salem and conferred with several leaders, including Egbert L. Davis, chairman of the Board of Trustees of the North Carolina Baptist Hospital, and Dr. Wingate Johnson, then president of the Board of Trustees of Wake Forest College and a leading physician on the staff of the Baptist Hospital. I found nothing but enthusiasm for the movement.

A conference on the matter was arranged by Mr. Mull for November 11, 1938. Those expected at the conference were the committee named in the will of the late Bowman Gray to designate the beneficiary of the fund for the establishment of a charitable project. Committee members were Mrs. Nathalie Bernard, widow of the late Bowman Gray, their two sons, Bowman Gray and Gordon Gray, the late Mr. Gray's brother, James A. Gray, former Governor O. Max Gardner, Dr. Kitchin, Mr. Mull, and I. Mr. Mull, Dr. Kitchin, Mr. James Gray, and I were the only ones able to attend the meeting.

At that meeting, Mr. Mull acquainted Mr. Gray with the failure of his efforts to induce the medical school commission to accept the fund for the University of North Carolina medical school. He then asked Mr. Gray if the committee would consider making the same offer to the Wake Forest College medical school. Mr. Gray asked Dr. Kitchin if Wake Forest, through the use of the fund, could develop a four-year medical school in Winston-Salem. Dr. Kitchin stated that it could be done. Mr. Gray then informed Dr. Kitchin that the fund amounted to about $600,000. Mr. Gray sensed a fall in Dr. Kitchin's enthusiasm and asked him why, on learning the amount of the fund, he appeared less certain that it could be done. Dr. Kitchin replied that he had understood that the fund was much larger and that the actual amount made him hesitate. Mr. Mull, Dr. Kitchin, and I were under the impression prior to that time the fund available amounted to over $5 million.

Mr. Gray informed us that he, as a member of the committee and not being a direct member of the family, would be guided largely by the desires of Bowman Gray, Jr., Gordon Gray, and Mrs. Bernard. He agreed to report to them the results of the conference.

In the latter part of July, 1939, Dr. Kitchin received a letter from James A. Gray, inviting him, Mr. Mull, and me to meet with him, Bowman Gray, Jr., and Gordon Gray for dinner on the evening of August 2, 1939. At that conference the entire matter was reviewed. Dr. Kitchin, Mr. Mull, and I agreed to accept the fund for Wake Forest College if it were offered.

James Gray, Bowman Gray, and Gordon Gray agreed to make the fund available to the Wake Forest College medical school, stating that they wanted it clearly understood that they, as individuals, by that action concluded their responsibility in the development of the school and that henceforth it would be the responsibility of Wake Forest College.

Accordingly, the following memorandum was sent to Dr. Kitchin:

> We understand that Wake Forest College is interested in expanding its Medical School from a two-year to a four-year school and desires to have such a four-year department located in a city where sufficient hospital facilities and clinical material are available, and in answer to your inquiry as to the possibility of the resources of the Bowman Gray Fund in Winston-Salem Foundation being made available for your college in such a development, provided the four-year Medical School is established in Winston-Salem, and assuming that Wake Forest College can arrange to use as its college hospital the facilities of the North Carolina Baptist Hospital located in Winston-Salem, we advise as follows:
>
> With the understanding that the Medical School will be conducted as an integral part of Wake Forest College, and with the further understanding that all funds that may be received from the Bowman Gray Fund in the Winston-Salem Foundation will be used exclusively for purposes of buildings and operations of the School of Medicine in Winston-Salem, the undersigned, authorized under the will of the late Bowman Gray to designate the use of the above mentioned funds, will direct Wachovia Bank and Trust Company as Trustee of the Winston-Salem Foundation to turn over all the resources of said Bowman Gray Fund to Wake Forest College for the purposes above enumerated.

The executive committee of the Board of Trustees of Wake Forest College and the executive committee of the Board of Trustees of the North Carolina Baptist Hospital met simultaneously at 4:00 p.m. on August 3, 1939. The executive committee of the college voted to accept the proposal and move the medical school to Winston-Salem, and the executive committee of the hospital board voted to make the facilities of the Baptist Hospital available to the medical school and to enlarge the hospital and provide financial support to meet the needs of a first-class four-year medical school. Public announcement of the action was made through the daily press of the state the following day, Sunday, August 4, 1939.

Wingate M. Johnson
Professor of clinical medicine and president of the Board of Trustees when the Bowman Gray School of Medicine was founded in 1939

Chapter 3

The Four-Year School

Getting Started in Winston-Salem

Several studies had been made of the minimum amount of money required to build a creditable four-year medical school, and $10 million was the amount commonly considered to be needed. A portion of this amount would be provided through the Bowman Gray bequest of approximately $600,000 (18,500 shares of R. J. Reynolds Tobacco Company "B" Common stock) and the annual support of $22,450 provided by the Board of Trustees for the existing two-year school. Why did the representatives of the college agree to assume the undertaking without more adequate financial assurance? The fact that the project was undertaken was severely criticized by leaders in medical education, with the exception of Dr. Fred C. Zapffe, secretary of the Association of American Medical Colleges, who was always helpful and encouraging. The one word that explains our action is "faith." Repeatedly I have said that, "Faith in God and man and hard work made us succeed."

When Dr. Kitchin and I were driving to Winston-Salem for the conference at which it was agreed to accept the challenge, Dr. Kitchin said, "Carpenter, I have thought this thing through, and I have decided that we should accept the offer from the Grays, if made, no matter how small the amount of money, because I have complete faith that ultimately adequate financial support will be found."

Near the conclusion of our conference in Winston-Salem, Mr. Gordon Gray turned to me and said, "You are the person who will have to do the job. What do you think of the possibilities of success in the face of the small financial support?" The answer to that question was weighed carefully. To agree to go forward would be accepting tremendous responsibility. I said, "We'll succeed, because we will not spend money we don't have." Trying to live up to that commitment has caused many hours of anxiety.

A short time after the agreement was reached, Dr. Kitchin went to New York to solicit additional support from the Rockefeller Foundation. He was thoroughly discouraged by Dr. Alan Gregg, medical director of the foundation, and was advised to use the $600,000 to strengthen the premedical departments at Wake Forest. Of course, Dr. Gregg's advice could not be followed because the Gray gift was for a four-year medical school in Winston-Salem, so Dr. Kitchin returned with no money and many words of discouragement.

The Development of Medical Facilities

It was felt that the two-year school at Wake Forest comprised a good nucleus for the first two years of a four-year medical school. Facilities for the last two years had to be developed from the beginning. An adequate number of properly distributed hospitals beds came first on the list of requirements.

Initial efforts were directed toward unifying all hospital and medical facilities in Winston-Salem and Forsyth County under one program for care of the sick, education, and advancement of the knowledge of the science of medicine. This effort largely failed. The failure, it is sad to say, was due to jealousies, selfishness, and lack of vision on the part of many people. When this failure became evident, in order to meet the needs of the medical school, the Baptist Hospital Board of Trustees voted in 1940 to double the number of beds to be added, making a total addition of two hundred beds.

The Baptist Hospital, on July 1, 1950, had a bed capacity of three hundred, an outpatient clinic building taking care of approximately forty thousand patient visits a year, an emergency clinic, a school of nursing, and training facilities for eighty-six interns and residents. The additional clinical facilities consisted of a clinic for private patients, operated in the medical school, the Methodist Children's

Bowman Gray III, right,
and Egbert L. Davis III
break ground to start
the new Bowman Gray School of Medicine
and expansion of North Carolina Baptist Hospital.

Home, Graylyn (neuropsychiatric hospital), and several clinics in outlying districts of Forsyth and adjoining counties.

The Bowman Gray School of Medicine building was constructed adjacent to North Carolina Baptist Hospital and actually constituted one wing of the hospital-medical school building. Construction was begun in 1940 and was completed in time for classes to begin in September, 1941. Forty-five students were accepted from five hundred applicants for the first-year class. They, with thirty second-year students from the old campus, comprised the student body for the school's first year in Winston-Salem.

The building was intended to provide facilities for the expanded first two years of a medical school. Until facilities for the school could be expanded, we planned to use the same space for the Private Diagnostic Clinic, offices for the faculty, and classrooms and research laboratories for the third and fourth year.

The plan was to add to the building, but the movement to relocate Wake Forest College in Winston-Salem prevented us from going ahead with that plan. Plans for additional expansion of the Baptist Hospital also were postponed. As a consequence, in 1950 the medical school and the Baptist Hospital were greatly overcrowded.

Between the time of the 1946 decision to move Wake Forest College to Winston-Salem and 1956 when it was moved, the medical school and hospital faced tremendous problems of raising funds for expansion and, at the same time, avoiding competition with the parent institution. In spite of these difficulties some expansion was provided to include additions to both the hospital and medical school. The expansion provided, however, continued to lag behind the needs for teaching, research, and patient care. It was not until the beginning of the $30 million expansion program in 1963, that adequate facilities for the rapidly growing and developing medical center could be visualized.

From the beginning, in the care of patients, we adopted two policies: (1) every patient coming to the hospital, regardless of ability to pay, is available for teaching purposes; (2) patients financially able to pay the Department of Clinics a physician's fee shall do so under a medical service plan for full-time faculty operated by the medical school.

The philosophy behind these policies was: (1) students, when they become physicians, will treat patients of different economic levels, so they should have experience with the approach to private paying patients (which is usually with more concern for the niceties) as well as charity patients; (2) patients financially able to pay should not be discriminated against, and the services of exceptionally well qualified physicians should be made available to them; (3) it conserves the time of the clinician to have all his activities under one roof; (4) the income from private patients is a valuable asset in financial support of the clinical faculty.

I have often said that the original faculty that formed the Department of Clinics was one of the most important contributions to the success of the medical school. The majority were physicians, already located in Winston-Salem, who had no idea before it was announced that the Wake Forest medical school would be moved to Winston-Salem or that they would become a part of the clinical faculty of a medical school. Some of these physicians are still members of the faculty and have developed national prestige of leadership and a reputation for unusual excellence in their chosen fields of medicine. The type of physician located in Winston-Salem is a great tribute to the quality of the medical profession in this relatively small southern city.

The original group was composed of the following physicians: Dr. Leroy Butler, professor and chairman, Department of Pediatrics; Dr. Fred K. Garvey, assistant professor in charge of urology; Dr. Robert Garvey, urologist; Dr. James A. Harrill, assistant professor in charge of otorhinolaryngology; Dr. Wingate M. Johnson, clinical professor of medicine and chief of the Private Diagnostic Clinic; Dr. Elbert A. MacMillan, assistant professor of clinical medicine and clinical psychiatry; Dr. Robert L. McMillan, associate professor of clinical medicine and chief of cardiology; Dr. Robert A. Moore, associate professor of surgery in charge of orthopedics; Dr. James P. Rousseau, professor and chairman, Department of Radiology; Dr. William H. Sprunt, professor of clinical surgery; Dr. Arthur Valk, professor of clinical surgery; Dr. Roscoe L. Wall, assistant professor of surgery in charge of anesthesiology.

The value of these twelve doctors in the development of the school cannot be overestimated. They will always have my unreserved gratitude.

Selection of the Staff

A new medical school without adequate funds or attractive reputation has one of three possibilities for additions to the staff: (1) young men who visualize the new school as an opportunity to get ahead rapidly; (2) people with ability and scientific reputation who are dissatisfied with their positions; (3) able and reputable alumni and friends of the institution who are sufficiently loyal to sacrifice and take chances on the future in order to contribute to the school's development. The faculty members selected fell into each of the three groups. As would be expected, the majority of those who remained on the faculty were from group one or group three.

The faculty of the Bowman Gray School of Medicine is unique. It is a mixture of dedicated men of science, teachers and leaders of students, and competent people in the field of medical care. It is customary to point out leaders, but one cannot say with finality that certain members of the faculty exceed others in their contributions. The following are outstanding illustrations of the different types referred to above. The order in which they appear is of no significance.

Dr. Herbert M. Vann, professor of anatomy, was a stalwart figure in both stages of the school. He taught anatomy, except for an interval of eighteen months, from 1919 until his death from coronary disease in 1951. His portrait was presented to the School as a tribute of love by his colleagues and former students and occupies a prominent place in the library. At ceremonies held when this portrait was unveiled, Dr. Wingate Johnson, then acting dean of the school while I was on leave, said:

> For more than a quarter of a century he had taught anatomy to successive generations of students at the medical school of Wake Forest College—first when it was a two-year school, and later when it was expanded to a four-year school and moved to Winston-Salem.
>
> Dr. Vann taught much more than the dry facts of anatomy. From him students learned respect for the human body and its Maker; they learned that medicine is a jealous but a just mistress. As for their teacher, they learned first to fear "The Major" as he was generally known, then to admire him, and finally to love him as few of their teachers were loved. They learned that he was their friend, who would do anything that he honorably could to help them. After they graduated from medical school and finished their hospital training, they looked upon him as a connecting link between them and their Alma Mater. As permanent secretary of the Wake Forest Medical Alumni Association and chairman of the Library Fund, he kept in touch with all his former students, and they with him.
>
> His colleagues learned that he could be depended upon to carry out any task assigned him, and to do it cheerfully. As a result, when the end came, the question, "Who will take his place?" was quickly amended to "Who will take his places?"

Dr. Camillo Artom, professor of biochemistry, was a dedicated researcher and scientist brought from the University of Palermo in Italy to the two-year school at Wake Forest in 1937. His great scientific contributions were recognized in those days, particularly his work in lipids. Dr. Emmett Holt, Jr., professor of pediatrics at Johns Hopkins, had a similar interest. On hearing of our need for a new professor of biochemistry, Dr. Holt strongly recommended Dr. Artom as a person who was available.

I wrote to every chairman of a department of biochemistry in all of the medical schools in the United States, and all of the replies were astonishingly complimentary. There was some amazement that Wake Forest, a little-known school in those days, was able to attain such a great scientist. By the time he began his work at Wake Forest, he had been offered three other positions in nationally known institutions, but his gratitude to Wake Forest for making it possible for him to come to America to continue his work was so great that he would not consider much finer positions with much higher salaries. After his retirement, Dr. Artom continued his research with dedication in spite of many frustrating illnesses. His spirit of humility and generosity toward people created in our institution a great tradition of working co-operatively. Dr. Artom died February 3, 1970.

Dr. Wingate Johnson, professor of clinical medicine, may be called a medical philosopher. He was known as a scholar not in medicine alone. He was located in Winston-Salem in the practice of internal medicine many years before the school was moved from Wake Forest. The committee, in awarding him an honorary degree from Wake Forest College, debated whether to offer him the degree of Doctor of Science or Doctor of Literature. Dr. Johnson joined the faculty on the opening of the medical school in 1941. He had served as a member of the Wake Forest Board of Trustees for twenty years and was its chairman at the time. He was the Osler type of teacher who inspired his students and led them to appreciate the philosophy of the Great Physician.

The election of Dr. Tinsley Harrison as the first professor and chairman of the Department of Medicine, like the election of Dr. Artom, brought to the institution a national image that was greatly needed at the time. Dr. Harrison came to the medical school from the faculty of the Vanderbilt University School of Medicine. He left the Bowman Gray faculty in March 1944 to become the first dean of the

Southwestern Medical School of the University of Texas. He has continued to be one of the great scholars of medicine in this country.

Dr. Robert P. Morehead, professor and chairman of the Department of Pathology, illustrates a type referred to above as a loyal son of Wake Forest who is dedicated to giving his all to his Alma Mater. While carrying a tremendous load of teaching, research, and practice of pathology, he brought himself up by his own bootstraps to become one of the most highly respected men in his field. He not only spent many years in perfecting his knowledge of man in health and disease, he also spent many years in writing a textbook, entitled *Human Pathology*, that was published in 1965 and is widely used throughout the medical world.

Dr. Howard Holt Bradshaw, professor and chairman of the Department of Surgery, was the first man elected to a professorship and as chairman of a clinical department on the establishment of the Bowman Gray School of Medicine. He was a young man who had spent ten years in research and postgraduate study after his graduation from medical school. He was best known for his leadership in surgical education and the training of interns and residents in surgery. He had wide connections and served on many boards and committees in medical education. His residency training program produced many highly competent and well-trained young surgeons. He died August 11, 1969.

Dr. Frank R. Lock, professor and chairman of the Department of Obstetrics and Gynecology, also was a first in the development of a four-year medical school faculty. He was among the youngest of the men selected to chair a department. He came to the Bowman Gray School of Medicine following a fellowship at Tulane University School of Medicine.

Two interesting features characterize Dr. Lock. He never claimed to be an individual competent in basic research, but his ability to assemble teachers of the highest quality in basic research was phenomenal. He is also a great clinician, and it was Dr. Lock who brought to the institution the idea of a program in behavioral sciences. This program has become one of the best-known features of the educational program. The program is headed by Dr. Clark Vincent who is nationally known in the field and who has been joined by Dr. David Mace and others in this large and humanitarian project.

There is not an honor of distinction in the field of obstetrics and gynecology that Dr. Lock has not received. He is the only man in America to serve as president of both the American College of Obstetricians and Gynecologists and American Association of Obstetricians and Gynecologists at the same time. He served as president of the American Gynecological Society during the 1967–68 year.

Dr. James A. Harrill, professor and director of the Section on Otolaryngology, was among the Winston-Salem physicians who joined the faculty in 1941. He was graduated from the two-year Wake Forest College School of Medicine, from the University of Pennsylvania, and has received extensive and outstanding postgraduate training. As one of the faculty members I have classified as a loyal Wake Forest alumnus, he has brought national distinction to the school through his own work and the development of his department.

Interestingly enough, in 1941 when we asked local physicians who should head otolaryngology, Dr. Harrill was named by every one, including members of his own field who might be competitors for the position. This is a fine tribute to any young physician, and for Jimmy Harrill it was doubly so because, at the time, he had been in practice in Winston-Salem for only three years.

Dr. Frederick K. Garvey, professor and director of the Section on Urology and an outstanding clinician and scientist in his field, is another of the men practicing medicine in Winston-Salem when the medical school was moved to the city. Like Dr. Harrill, he immediately was deemed the one qualified to head a department in a four-year medical school. Like Dr. Lock, he surrounded himself with outstanding and well-qualified research men. His own research, particularly in the field of the formation of kidney and bladder stones, is recognized nationally and internationally. Dr. Garvey retired from the faculty at his own request on May 1, 1969.

Since the beginning of my tenure as dean, I have believed that one of the most important things an administrator can do regarding sound continuity of development is to surround himself with able people who can carry on once he is removed either by retirement or death. I often said that my ideal would be to develop administration in such a way that my dropping out would not be noticed. I was fortunate in doing just that.

Dr. Manson Meads has a fine background in education, scientific attainment, and proven ability in administration. He came to the Bowman Gray School of Medicine from a series of important appointments at Harvard Medical School where he served as resident at Thorndike Memorial Laboratory, assistant in medicine at Boston City Hospital, and assistant in bacteriology and Ernst Fellow in bacteriology. His first appointment at the Bowman Gray School of Medicine in 1947 was as instructor in medicine. He served from 1948 to 1953 as a Markle Scholar in medical sciences. He progressed through assistant and associate professorships to professor and chairman of the Department of Preventive Medicine in 1955, after having taken leave for two years to serve as a special consultant in medicine to Siriraj and Chulalongkorn Medical Schools in Bangkok, Thailand. On his return I induced him to become associate dean in 1955. He served as associate dean, academic dean, executive dean, and dean and became vice president for medical affairs and dean of medicine on July 1, 1967, the date of my retirement.

It has been said that one of the greatest things for progress is to have the man and the hour coincide. When Dr. Meads became dean, he produced the type of leadership that was basically mandatory for the Bowman Gray School of Medicine to continue a forward thrust. He has brought together the newly developing medical center with wisdom, judgment, and smoothness of administration that probably could not be surpassed. His vast knowledge of the operation of medical schools and the medical divisions of the U.S. government has caused him to be appointed to many important committees, boards, and commissions. He serves at present as consultant, Review Committee, Bureau of Health Manpower in Washington.

The faculty members listed here are used as illustrations of the general type and variations in interests of members of the faculty. Many others have served with equal distinction, but space will not permit including all who deserve mention.

Again, I must apologize for a personal reference, but administration should be included. I am fortunate, however, not to have to write my own "obituary." The following was written by the late Dr. Wingate Johnson.

"Dr. Coy C. Carpenter was Dr. Kitchin's right-hand man during the last decade the school was at Wake Forest, and played a leading role in his election as president of the college. His greatest contribution to the school, however, was in the transition from a two-year school of medical sciences to the present full-fledged four-year medical school. Suffice it to say here that his faith, his optimism, his courage, his diplomatic skill, his energy, and his foresight played a great part in the accomplishment of a task which leaders in medical education said was impossible. Dr. Carpenter, like Napoleon, regarded an obstacle as something to be overcome.

"In evaluating his administrative achievements, Dr. Carpenter's professional accomplishments should not be forgotten. Even before the medical school was moved from Wake Forest, he and his colleague, Dr. R. P. Morehead, had won a wide reputation for their work in pathology, and many of the smaller hospitals in the state and surrounding states depended upon him and Dr. Morehead for the solution of their pathologic problems. After the expansion of the school to four years, the material sent by these hospitals served a twofold purpose of supplying students with good teaching material and of making the Department of Pathology self-supporting. Dr. Carpenter's standing as a pathologist was recognized by his selection as a Fulbright Visiting Professor to Cairo in 1953–1954."

Students

The student body at the medical school on the Wake Forest campus was composed largely of native North Carolinians. Wake Forest College at that time had a very large premedical department, and there was no problem of filling the classes with our own graduates. When the school was moved to Winston-Salem, the premedical training at Wake Forest became less and less a major activity of the sciences. In keeping with the times, many students who were interested in sciences and formerly went into medicine now go into many of the newer scientific disciplines. So through the years the distribution of the residence of the student body has become more varied. In 1968 in the freshman class there were forty students from different colleges throughout the nation and only ten from Wake Forest. This again is in keeping with the newer methods of traveling and closer communication between different parts of the country and the world.

The quality of the students has always been good. For many years the dean of the University of Pennsylvania medical school kept records of all transfer students from two-year schools, and Wake Forest was usually in the top of the class. When the first class graduated from the four-year Bowman Gray School of Medicine, two of the top three scores made on the examinations leading to a license to practice medicine in North Carolina were made by students from that class. Another factor that helped internationalize the reputation of the Bowman Gray School of Medicine has been the fine record that our graduates have made in their internship and residency years. We would invariably receive the comment from the physicians on the staffs of the hospitals where they interned that "graduates of the Bowman Gray School of Medicine are different in that they know how to practice medicine." A summary of the number of applicants and quality and distribution of the applicants appears in table 1.

Table 1. Applicant Quality and Distribution: Summary figures.

	1948	1952	1958	1963	1968
Number applicants	1107	741	861	663	1087
Number admitted	55	54	55	55	61
Quality point ratio	2.1	2.2	2.1	2.0	2.2
*MCAT verbal		486	451	499	520
MCAT quantitative		481	480	536	580
MCAT general information		472	440	545	548
MCAT science		473	464	529	582
Number states represented	10	14	14	16	19
Number foreign countries	0	0	3	0	1
Number North Carolina residents	44	23	31	30	23
Number colleges	12	24	27	27	40
Number Wake Forest students	38	22	18	8	10

* Medical College Admission Test

Educational Policy and Curriculum

It has been said that "there is nothing new except that which has been forgotten." At the begining of the 1969 school year, Dr. Robert Tuttle, academic dean, announced on behalf of the faculty a new and modernized curriculum which would give students an introduction to patients during the first year of the four-year course.

In 1945 I reported to the Association of American Medical Colleges in a paper entitled "Experiments in Medical Education and Medical Care in a New Medical School." The paper was based on four years of experience with a new curriculum, and it said in part: "Appropriate cases illustrating the importance of the care of the sick patient are presented throughout the courses in anatomy, biochemistry, physiology, pathology, bacteriology, pharmacology, and laboratory diagnosis by the clinician as a member of the staff of the fundamental science concerned. In the junior and senior years the process is reversed. Members of the staff whose major interest is in a fundamental science make ward rounds with students, give lectures, and hold conferences with clinical clerks (third and fourth year students)." I also pointed out that traditional departmental barriers had been eliminated. Dr. Victor Johnson, secretary of the Council on Medical Education of the American Medical Association, then told the assembled medical school deans that all of them knew this was the proper way to organize a faculty and teach medical students, but they were unable to do so because of deeply ingrained tradition.

In 1969 the brilliant president of Wake Forest University, James Ralph Scales, discussing the problems faced by a university president dealing with students determined to control the university, reminded me that students are no more determined than faculty intellectuals. In 1945 we did not properly weigh the inclination of faculty members to view with alarm and label as low quality education any threat to intrude on their basic intellectual concepts. I fear that today it may be hard to overcome a similar lack of appreciation of the depth of human desire to promote the individual point of view. One basic science department at the medical school already has viewed the new (1969) interdisciplinary course in "The Cellular Basis of Medicine" as lacking sufficient depth to meet their educational standards. The "new" curiculum of 1945 did not completely collapse, but the threat of erosion is always present.

The establishment of a new medical school presents an unparalleled opportunity for progress in medical education. That fact is not as true today as it was in 1941 when the Bowman Gray School of Medicine opened its doors. Prior to that time, this country's established medical schools had done very little deviating from the traditional curriculum. The newer disciplines in medicine had only begun, and, in general, the established schools had made little progress toward getting out of the rut of traditional educational patterns. Subject emphasis often was influenced by the pressures and authority that could be commanded by various departmental directors.

With the opening of the new school, the faculty of the Bowman Gray School of Medicine started a long-range experiment in medical education and medical care. The general philosophy centered around the elimination of rigid departmental barriers in education and research. There was also a program designed to provide a more appropriate balance in subject emphasis.

The Bowman Gray School of Medicine began the policy of virtually eliminating the traditional departments as such. It was decided that the study of medicine, which is the study of man in health and disease, could be conveniently divided into four sections:

(1) A division relating to normal man and the common disorders of structure and function which result from disease, injury, or defect. This division encompassed the traditional departments of anatomy, pathology, and radiology.

(2) A division which included the traditional departments of physiology, biochemistry, and pharmacology.

(3) The division of medicine, which included internal medicine, preventive medicine, pediatrics and bacteriology.

(4) The division of surgery, which consisted of all surgery including the specialties.

I delivered a paper on our plan, titled "Integration and Organization of the Medical Curriculum," before the Association of American Medical Colleges meeting in Edgewater Park, Mississippi in 1946. The conclusions of the paper follow.

CONCLUSIONS

1. Medical knowledge has become so extensive that, without well-planned integration and correlation of the teaching program, the specialties tend to become isolated and the curriculum unbalanced.

2. The Bowman Gray School of Medicine of Wake Forest College has experimented with integration and organization for five years. The plans of horizontal and vertical correlation which are followed at present have been outlined and discussed.

3. After five years, the plan as outlined is obtaining results which are gratifying to both faculty members and students.

Since that time, many new and progressive educational policies and curriculums have been modified and improved in this country. The Bowman Gray School of Medicine has continued to liberalize and experiment with the curriculum, adding to and including the several scientific disciplines that have developed.

When the medical school library was moved from Wake Forest, it consisted of less than 2,500 volumes. By 1957 it contained more than 18,500 volumes and about 525 journals representing all branches of medicine. By 1968 the total volumes reached 52,168, and the journal subscription was 1,277. The library now is linked through a teletype network with a growing list of medical libraries.

The library is located on the first and ground floors of the medical school building. On the first floor is the well-lighted, air conditioned reading room, handsomely furnished with tables and chairs and lined with shelves containing books and periodicals. A stairway and an elevator provide ready access to six floors of stacks. To maintain the library, certain special funds augment the general fund of the school.

The greatest boost for support of the library came in 1960 when the R. J. Reynolds Tobacco Company gave $125,000 for volumes and the Z. Smith Reynolds Foundation gave $75,000. This made possible the increase of the volumes from 21,500 to 35,000. Library policy has always been to accept and catalogue only material of high quality and functional use. Accepting materials of questionable value for the sake of quoting a large number of volumes has never been done.

Dark Days

The period 1943 through 1945 may correctly be classed as "dark days." In spite of constant effort, no substantial additional financial support had been found. The minimum financial demands for a first-class school had passed available income. The college launched a campaign for $6 million for expansion, but there was no disposition to allow any of the amount raised for the medical school. President Kitchin maintained the position that when the school was moved to Winston-Salem, agreement was reached that the college would spend no more on the medical school than had been spent the year before removal of the two-year school at Wake Forest. This support amounted to the nominal sum of $22,450. I knew of no such agreement.

The situation was felt in the community of Winston-Salem and in the faculty. At the same time professional and church prejudice against the new school was at its height. The "Town and Gown" difficulties were constantly fanned by a few dissidents. Some of the conservative and fundamentalist Baptists expected the medical center to operate with more regard for church dogmàs than interest in the advancement of scientific medical research and education. The morale of the faculty was at its worst; faculty members claimed that deceitful tactics had been used to induce them to come on the faculty of a school with insufficient funds to operate, and several left.

Graylyn—A Mistake

During the early years, after the acceptance of the challenge to develop a complete four-year school, we took many gambles. A little money gained here and there was just enough to stave off bankruptcy. Gambles are taken on faith and hope. Our biggest gamble was the acceptance of the large and expensive Bowman Gray estate, Graylyn.

Gifts of Graylyn were spread over several years. The estate at the beginning of this period consisted of approximately ninety-nine acres of land, a group of farm buildings, a small cottage, a greenhouse, an eight-room residence, and the larger manor house of about forty rooms. The houses and greenhouse, including the largest portion of the land, were donated by Mrs. Bernard. Other segments of the land previously divided into lots were donated by Mr. Gray's two sons.

The first gift of Graylyn was made by Mrs. Bernard on the occasion of the opening of the Bowman Gray School of Medicine on September 10, 1941. This gift consisted of the farm buildings valued at $250,000. It included two living quarters for workers on the estate as well as space for farm and garden activities.

It was hoped that these facilities could be developed into a research institute. In 1941, unlike today, no government funds were available to us for research. Medical school research programs were supported by the private foundations, largely the Rockefeller Foundation. The foundations, in part seeking their own aggrandizement, favored the support of prestige schools. Wake Forest obviously at that time was far from being a prestige school. At any rate the so-called Research Institute of the Bowman Gray School of Medicine was never able to find financial support to "get off the ground."

In 1946 Mrs. Bernard included the manor house in her donation of a part of the Graylyn estate to be used as a psychiatry hospital. She also donated $60,000 for equipment, and Gordon Gray donated $125,000 to be used $25,000 per year for deficit financing during the first five years of operation. Bowman Gray donated a like amount for deficit financing to start a department of preventive medicine.

Graylyn Hospital was opened the middle of August and was formally dedicated September 19, 1947. It was operated as a psychiatric hospital until January 1, 1959. Since that date all psychiatric patient care and the Department of Psychiatry have been located in the medical center. This brought all teaching, research, and patient care under one roof.

Graylyn has been used for many activities, but it has continued for the most part as a center for mental health. At present this consists of four units: (1) Amos Cottage for custodial care, teaching, and research in mental retardation, (2) the Pediatric Developmental Evaluation Clinic, (3) Graylyn Children's Center for Psychology, Reading, and Speech, and (4) the Children's Center for the Handicapped.

In addition, there are twenty living units for faculty and other institution personnel at Graylyn.

Need for Development of a University

A medical school cannot offer a satisfactory program at the Master's and Ph.D. degree levels without integration with the arts and sciences of a college or university. While on the campus of Wake Forest College, even as a small two-year medical school, we found the interrelation between the Schools of Arts and Sciences and the School of Medicine to be a basic need. Moving to Winston-Salem we quickly realized that such a lack of association and integration of courses was a great loss.

In 1940, when the medical school left the Wake Forest campus, both the college and the medical school offered the Master's degree. During World War II the college developed a student body out of proportion to a satisfactory student-faculty ratio and was forced to drop the graduate program, but the medical school continued to offer the Master's degree.

In 1961 the college re-established a Division of Graduate Studies. The medical school in the meantime had progressed to the point of offering the Ph.D. degree. The university's graduate school now offers study and research leading to the Master's in twelve departments, and the medical school offers work for both the Master's and Ph.D. degrees.

Finances

Funds to construct and equip the new building in Winston-Salem were borrowed from the National Shawmut Bank of Boston. The 18,500 shares of R. J. Reynolds Tobacco Company "B" stock, plus 300 shares purchased through a $10,000 gift from Mrs. Ida Charlton, were used as collateral. The money was borrowed at 1 percent interest.

During the war years the operation of the school twelve months in the year, with a new class admitted every nine months, made the income from tuition offset the lack of endowment. The school income in 1941 was $184,774.70, of which $33,209.32 was from student fees. The income for 1944 was $338,820.28, of which $108,004.51 was from student fees. This situation plus income through various auxiliary enterprises enabled us to keep income above expenditures. Endowment income remains approximately $44,000 per year.

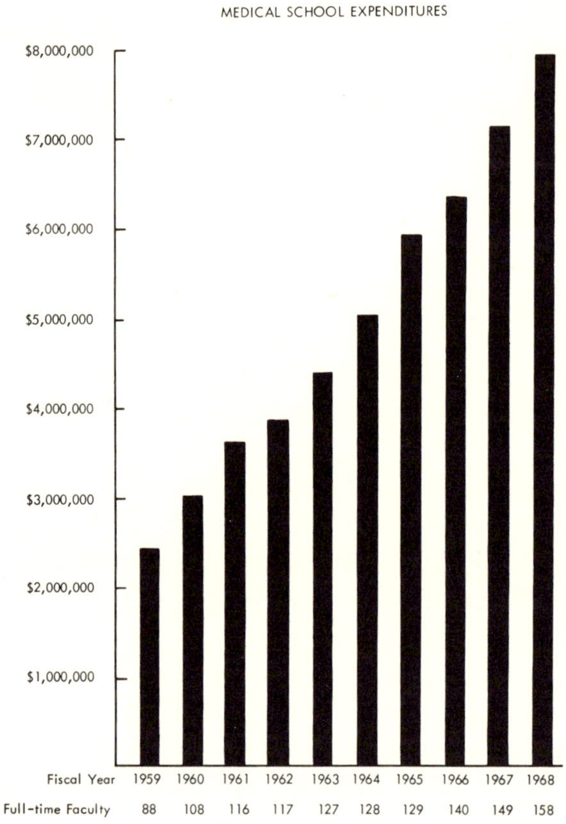

Fig. 1

A big change in funds available for medical education has taken place during the last thirty years, and the Bowman Gray School of Medicine has experienced the change. Before the days of heavy taxation for education, the poor schools were the state supported schools. I recall about thirty years ago hearing the late G. Lombard Kelly, then dean of the University of Georgia medical school, almost tearfully making a talk before the Association of American Medical Colleges on the plight of the poor state-supported medical school. The private schools were better off financially because of the better returns from endowment. With the advent of heavy taxation and the federal government's entrance into the field of medical research and medical assistance, the pendulum swung back, and finances came in greater and greater percentages from government-sponsored programs, research, and training grants. In 1968 some schools found that as high as 70 percent of their expenditures came through government sponsored programs. This is a handicap because of the scarcity of unrestricted funds. The trends in the Bowman Gray School of Medicine are similar.

Development Program

A modest expansion of the Bowman Gray School of Medicine and North Carolina Baptist Hospital has taken place during the last several years. The James A. Gray Building, the Research Center Building with one addition, and two expansions of the hospital have taken place since 1941.

The tremendous 1969 expansion program was the first large building program attempted by the medical center. The last phase of the program, scheduled for completion in 1971, will increase the size of the medical center by 80 percent and will cost approximately $30 million. Major elements of the program are the Hanes Building, a 122,000-square-foot addition to the medical school; the Charles H. Babcock Auditorium; a 16-story hospital and clinics building, the hospital expansion, including the Reynolds Patient Tower that will boost the hospital's bed complement to 695 teaching beds; a 55,500-square-foot building which is now the instructional center for the allied health programs; and a new power plant.

The expansion has enabled the medical school to increase the number of students in each entering class to seventy-six. Fifty-four first-year medical students were accepted each year prior to 1967 when the size of the first-year class was expanded to sixty-one.

As a result of the expansion program, as well as the reorganization of paramedical education programs, more and newer types of allied health personnel will train at the medical center. Table 2 reflects anticipated increases in the various paramedical programs.

Except for nursing and pastoral care, all programs listed in table 2 are now part of the medical school's Division of Allied Health Programs established in 1969 for the purpose of upgrading and coordinating paramedical education, investigating new areas in which allied health personnel might serve productively, developing curriculums that will assure proper training for students in new paramedical disciplines, and increasing the production of trained personnel for health team responsibilities. New programs have been established for the training of physician assistants and nuclear medicine technicians.

Table 2. Paramedical Programs: Reflection of growth.

Program	*1965 Enrollment*	*Expanded Enrollment*
Nursing	174	300
Radiological technology	21	30
Nurse anesthetists	20	30
Inhalation therapy	11	24
Medical technology	19	24
Medical records administration	12	20
Pastoral care (Seminar Gp)	20	25
Pastoral care (1-yr. Interns)	10	16
Cytotechnology	4	8
Physical therapy	0	10
Totals	291	487

Board of Visitors

The Board of Visitors plan used by Wake Forest University originated when the medical school was moved to Winston-Salem, and a permanent advisory council was created to advise on financial matters and the over-all development of the school. The council consisted of the committee designated in the will of the late Bowman Gray to select the beneficiary of the fund that had been awarded to the school. The committee functioned largely through James A. Gray.

The late James A. Gray was an outstanding Methodist layman. As the brother of the late Bowman Gray, whom he greatly admired, Mr. Gray always felt and demonstrated a keen attachment to the Bowman Gray School of Medicine. He advised me constantly and unselfishly in all matters pertaining to the school. In matters financial I relied on him heavily. From 1939 until his death in 1952 he was my greatest inspiration and help. He was never too busy to see and help me in spite of his heavy responsibilities as president and chairman of the board of the R. J. Reynolds Tobacco Company and his many church and community activities. His $900,000 gift to the school on January 1, 1947, was the first substantial financial support the school received. Mr. James A. Gray without question was the one person most responsible for saving the school from financial failure.

As chairman and spokesman for this original committee, and through his naturally respected business abilities, James Gray was able

James A. Gray

to obtain a loan from the National Shawmut Bank of Boston for the construction and equipment of the Bowman Gray School of Medicine at 1 percent interest. This one act made possible the construction of the school, and through economies and good business management the Bowman Gray School of Medicine never had to liquidate a single dollar of the original Bowman Gray bequest. The original $600,000 has been retained and at present has a market value of approximately $3 million depending on the stock market fluctuations.

The present Board of Visitors of the medical school has provided the leadership for raising $30 million for the expansion of the medical center. Under the very able leadership of Mr. John Watlington, chairman of the Board of Visitors and president of the Wachovia Bank and Trust Company, this committee to date has raised almost $13 million from individuals, businesses, and foundations, and there is in sight almost $26 million of the $30 million required. They are putting on a new campaign and have assumed the responsibility of raising the remainder.

Without question the development program could not have become a reality without the leadership and work of the Board of Visitors. The campaign conducted by Mr. Watlington, with the assistance of the other members, has resulted in the realization of the following available funds:

Total Project Costs:	$29,932,876 (5/6/69)
Sources of Income	
Federal Agencies	
Health research facilities	$ 1,062,000
Medical education facilities	9,685,478
Hill-Burton facilities	2,000,000
	$12,747,478
Local Matching	
Pledges and cash to date	$12,877,621
Total income to date	$25,625,099
Balance of funds needed	$ 4,307,777

The amount raised by the Board of Visitors from individuals, corporations, and foundations in Winston-Salem surpassed by several million dollars any other similar effort.

In April, 1964 the Wake Forest University Board of Trustees established a Board of Visitors for the law school and a Board of Visitors for the School of Arts and Sciences including the business school. A separate Board of Visitors was established for the Charles H. Babcock School of Business on October 11, 1969.

The 1969 Board of Visitors of the Bowman Gray School of Medicine is composed of the following persons: Albert Butler, Jr., chairman; Mrs. Charles H. Babcock; Irving E. Carlyle; William B. Cash; Edwin Collette; William J. Conrad; James K. Glenn; Bowman Gray, III; James A. Gray, Jr.; Gordon Gray; P. Huber Hanes; Ralph Hanes; Dr. George W. Paschal; William Lybrook; Colin Stokes; and John Watlington, Jr.

Following are the guidelines for the Board of Visitors of the medical school that were adopted in 1965 "with the additional provision that two members of the Board of Visitors be chosen from the Executive Committee of the Board of Trustees." In January, 1969 provision was made that the chairman of the Board of Trustees of the North Carolina Baptist Hospital also be a member of the Board of Visitors.

Proposed Guidelines for the Board of Visitors of the Bowman Gray School of Medicine of Wake Forest College—Adopted by the Executive Committee of the Board of Trustees in Session September 17, 1965.

Background

The present plan has evolved out of the experience of 25 years, in recognizing and responding to the need and importance of effective counsel and guidance in meeting changing conditions in the growth of the Bowman Gray School of Medicine. In June 1940, Dean C. C. Carpenter recommended, ". . . that the original Committee named in the will of the late Bowman Gray for the designation of the original $600,000 be continued as a permanent Finance Committee of the Bowman Gray School of Medicine, to act in an advisory capacity only, in cooperation with the President of the College and the Dean of the Medical School."

The recommendation was adopted by the Trustees of Wake Forest College, thus creating the Advisory Council, to act as an aid to the Board of Trustees in the conduct of the Medical School, but not in any way as a substitute for the authority and responsibility of the Trustees. The members of the committee at that time were: Mr. Bowman Gray, Jr.; Mr. Gordon Gray; Mrs. Nathalie L. Bernard; and Mr. James A. Gray.

Upon the death of the late Mr. James A. Gray on October 29, 1952, Mr. Bowman Gray, Jr., succeeded to the chairmanship of the committee, and suggested that the committee be enlarged. This was done. In May 1955 the committee was composed of Messrs. Bowman Gray, Chairman; James A. Gray, Jr.; Charles H. Babcock; Albert Butler, Jr.; Irving E. Carlyle; William Conrad; James G. Hanes and Richard J. Reynolds. In October 1958, the name of the Advisory Council was changed to the

President Harold W. Tribble
and the Board of Trustees of Wake Forest College
at beginning of development
of new campus in Winston-Salem.

Board of Visitors. Since that date the Board has continued its splendid services to the Medical School, with changes from time to time in membership and with gradual but very significant development in plans for improving and strengthening the Medical School.

For this record of distinguished service by the Board of Visitors across the years, the Trustees of Wake Forest College register profound gratitude. The achievements of the past, the activities of the present, and the development program bear eloquent testimony to the value of such dedicated service.

The Trustees and administration of the College are especially grateful for the inspiring leadership manifested in making possible the establishment of our Medical Center and initially raising more than $8,700,000 toward the financing of the first phase of this very important project.

In suggesting guidelines for the continuing operation of the Board of Visitors, it is earnestly desired that we continue and conserve the spirit and operation of the plan as it has evolved out of the experiences of the past 25 years, and that we provide for modifications or developments in the plan in the years ahead. Hence it is desired that these guidelines combine a well-defined plan of operation with a measure of flexibility that will provide for such modifications as may be needed in the future.

Function of the Board of Visitors in Relation to the Board of Trustees

While the authority resides in the Board of Trustees and cannot be delegated, effectiveness of service requires that a functioning relationship between the Board of Visitors and the Board of Trustees be maintained in order to enable Wake Forest College and the School of Medicine to derive the maximum benefit from the service of both groups. To accomplish this, the following guidelines are proposed as a policy.

1. The Board of Visitors will continue to be constituted as at present, with nominations for membership being proposed or recommended by the Board of Visitors to the Board of Trustees from time to time, with the additional provision that two members of the Board of Visitors shall be chosen from the Executive Committee of the Board of Trustees.

2. The Board of Visitors will continue to concern itself with the development of the Medical School, including relations of the institution to the public and the medical profession, the solicitation of funds that may be required for the continued development of the institution, and the maintenance of adequate budget procedures.

3. The Board of Visitors will submit recommendations to the Executive Committee of the Trustees from time to time, and plans and policies for operation will in this manner be established, subject to approval of the Board of Trustees of Wake Forest College, the desired purpose being to eliminate confusion and expedite day-to-day operation at the maximum level of quality of service. For example, in the preparation of the budget of the Medical School the Dean and the Controller will annually submit a proposed budget to the Board of Visitors for study, thus enabling the

Board of Visitors to pass on regularly recommendations to the Board of Trustees.

4. The plan of operation of the Development Office at the Medical School will be as follows: the Dean and the Board of Visitors of the Medical School will submit a recommendation to the President of the College, who in turn will submit a recommendation to the Executive Committee of the Board of Trustees. The Director of Development at the Medical School will be responsible to the Dean of the Medical School, who is in turn responsible to the President of the College, who is under the authority of the Board of Trustees. The Dean of the Medical School will confer concerning these matters with the Board of Visitors and also with the President of the College. The Director of Development will confer with the Director of Development of Wake Forest College concerning plans and programs, and especially concerning campaigns for funds, in order to expedite correlation and collaboration between the Development Department of the College and the Development Department of the Medical School.

Medical School Scholarships

Ever since 1957 students at the Bowman Gray School of Medicine have received $150,000 annually in scholarships awarded by the Z. Smith Reynolds Foundation. This scholarship program is one of the greatest things that ever happened to the medical school and is one of the most generous contributions in medical education.

The purpose of the Reynolds Scholarship Program is to encourage bright young North Carolinians to study in the field of medicine. It has more than fulfilled this aim. The program has given us national prestige, and it has enabled us to attract some of the best young brains in the state to our school.

Eight of these Reynolds scholarships are awarded each year to North Carolina students who have been accepted for the first-year class. Each Reynolds Scholar receives an award of $4,000 for his first year of study, $4,500 for his second and his third years, and $5,000 for his fourth year. Scholarship winners are selected by members of the admissions committee and trustees of the Z. Smith Reynolds Foundation on the basis of character, scholarship, potential as physicians, and financial need.

The scholarships are designated as the Mary Reynolds Babcock Scholarship, the William Neal Reynolds Scholarship, the Nancy Susan Reynolds Scholarship, the Richard J. Reynolds Scholarship, the Robert Edward Lasater Scholarship, the Nancy Lybrook Lasater

Scholarship, the Walter R. Reynolds Scholarship, and the Lucy Reynolds Critz Scholarship.

The scholarship program was one proposed to the school by Richard J. Reynolds, Jr. It was not solicited by us. Reynolds came to us with the idea. It was his feeling that young men and women who chose medicine as a profession were penalized by the long period of study required. He wanted to set up scholarships liberal enough that the medical student need not postpone marriage and a family, for example, until the completion of his education. Because I knew there was so much need, I tried to persuade Mr. Reynolds to reduce the cash value of the scholarship so the $150,000 could be distributed among more students, but he wanted the scholarship grants to be generous enough that the medical students might be even with young people going into fields requiring less extensive preparation.

At the end of each academic year, a $1,000 prize is awarded to the outstanding senior Reynolds Scholar at the medical school. These requirements are laid down for the winner: "His character, personality, and academic standing should be such that is is potentially a doctor of the highest quality. His academic standing should be high but need not be the highest among the Reynolds Scholars. He should possess warmth of feeling for his fellow men. He should have the ability to inspire confidence."

In addition to the scholarship program, the Z. Smith Reynolds Foundation has established a distinguished lectureship series at the Bowman Gray School of Medicine. The Richard J. Reynolds Lectureship Program, established in 1965, is designed to bring at least four nationally prominent speakers to the medical school each year and to enrich the school's educational programs by promoting contact between the students and outstanding scientists and physicians.

Two other fine scholarship programs are offered at the medical school. The Charles Alva Strickland Fund Scholarships are awarded on the basis of merit and need. The Annie L. Cannon Christian Scholarships are awarded to students who intend to practice medicine as medical missionaries. Both the Strickland and Cannon scholarships may cover full tuition costs, and both are renewable.

Bowman Gray
School of Medicine-North Carolina Baptist
Hospital Medical Center, 1970

Chapter 4

Organization of the Medical Center

The organization of the medical center, composed of the Bowman Gray School of Medicine and North Carolina Baptist Hospital, represents one of several types of arrangements for medical school-teaching hospitals in which the medical school and teaching hospital are separately owned.

This type of organization obviously requires satisfactory working agreements between the hospital and the medical school. Above all, it requires a constant spirit of oneness with the attitudes of give-and-take and co-operation between the Boards of Trustees, officials, faculty, and staff of the total institution.

The agreement between the North Carolina Baptist Hospital and the Bowman Gray School of Medicine adopted by the respective Boards of Trustees has been revised only once. The original and revised agreements entitled "Memorandum of Understanding" are as follows:

Memorandum of Understanding
Between the
North Carolina Baptist Hospital
and
The Bowman Gray School of Medicine of Wake Forest College

With a view to the promotion of the best medical care, and the best in teaching medical students, nurses and interns, the Board of Trustees of the North Carolina Baptist Hospital and the Bowman Gray School of Medicine enter into the following agreement:

1. On and after July 1, 1940, the Bowman Gray School of Medicine shall become responsible for the professional services of the North Carolina Baptist Hospital. It is specifically understood that the Medical School is not to employ any person to serve in the capacity of an employee of the Hospital whose salary or wage is to be paid by the Hospital, or to make any financial obligation for which the Hospital or the Board of Trustees would be responsible. It shall be further understood that the North Carolina Baptist Hospital by this agreement relinquishes none of its independence as a separate institution operated by its Board of Trustees under the North Carolina Baptist State Convention.

2. The Administrator of the Hospital shall be appointed by the Board of Trustees, and have charge of the business administration of the Hospital and shall have control of and be responsible for all property and persons not having directly to do with the care of the patients, except as otherwise provided in this agreement. He shall serve as the main source of contact and information between the Hospital, School of Medicine and the Denomination of the State. The Administrator of the Hospital shall be directly responsible to the Board of Trustees of the North Carolina Baptist Hospital.

3. A Medical Director shall be appointed by the Board of Trustees of the Hospital after consultation and on recommendation of the Dean of the Bowman Gray School of Medicine. He shall be a member of the Faculty of the School of Medicine, and shall be responsible for the professional administration of the Hospital in the manner and to the extent hereinafter provided.

4. A Hospital Staff Executive Committee shall be appointed and composed of the following:

(a) The Medical Director of North Carolina Baptist Hospital
(b) The Administrator of North Carolina Baptist Hospital
(c) The Dean of the Bowman Gray School of Medicine
(d) The Chief of Surgery, who shall be a salaried teacher in School of Medicine
(e) The Chief of Medicine, who shall be a salaried teacher in School of Medicine
(f) The Two Physicians who are members of the Board of Trustees.

This Hospital Staff Executive Committee shall be advisory to the Medical Director and the Administrator of the Hospital, except as herein otherwise stated. Meetings of the Executive Committee shall be held at the North Carolina Baptist Hospital on call of the Chairman or by any two members. The Chairman of the Committee shall be the Dean of the School of Medicine, and the Secretary shall be the Administrator of the Hospital. Minutes of such meetings shall be kept in triplicate, one copy furnished promptly to the Administrator of the Hospital, one to the Board of Trustees, and one for the files of the School of Medicine.

5. All appointments to the Hospital Regular Attending Staff and Resident Medical Staff shall be made by the Board of Trustees. The Dean of the School of Medicine shall submit to the Board of Trustees a list of nominations for such appointments after such list has been approved by the Hospital Staff Executive Committee. The Board of Trustees may reject any of the nominations and call for other nominations, but the Board of Trustees agrees not to appoint anyone to the Regular Attending Staff except on nomination by the Dean after approval of the Hospital Staff Executive Committee. All appointments to the Hospital Visiting or Courtesy Staff shall be made by the Board of Trustees. Applicants for appointment to the Visiting Staff must fill out the application form supplied by the Medical Director and Administrator of the Hospital.

6. For sufficient cause either the Administrator of the Hospital or the Medical Director may prefer charges against any Resident or member of the Regular Attending Staff to the Hospital Staff Executive Committee. Such charges shall be considered by the Hospital Staff Executive Committee before whom the accused shall have a hearing. The recommendation of the Hospital Staff Executive Committee, with a copy of the charges, shall be submitted to the Board of Trustees for final action.

7. The Medical Director is granted the privilege of requesting the Board of Trustees to remove any of the following persons who may in the course of their duties at the North Carolina Baptist Hospital be guilty of neglect, misconduct, or general incompetency; his or her record to be forwarded through the Administrator of the Hospital. Superintendent of Nurses, Instructress of Nurses, Supervisor of Nurses, Head Nurses, Pupil Nurses, Dietitians, Orderlies, and etc. The Board of Trustees before reaching a decision will make such investigation as it may deem necessary.

8. The Administrator of the Hospital may make complaint directly to the Board of Trustees against any intern, any employee of the Hospital or any member of the Staff, or any person connected in any way with the professional services of the Hospital, but shall previously give the Medical Director reasonable notice in writing that he is going to make such complaint and shall file therewith particulars in order that the Medical Director may have reasonable time and opportunity to rectify the undesirable condition under his control.

9. The conduct of the Superintendent of Nurses, other Nurses, Dietitians, Orderlies and other helpers shall be under the control of the Administrator of the Hospital. In all matters pertaining to the care of patients, these persons shall obey instructions of the Professional Staff. Any breach of discipline or disobedience of orders from the persons in authority connected with the Professional service, on the part of the above named employees, must be reported to the Administrator of the Hospital through the Medical Director. If the Administrator defaults proper action in such matters they may be laid by the Medical Director before the Hos-

pital Staff Executive Committee which may make such recommendations as it deems necessary to the Board of Trustees.

10. The Professional Staff shall be divided into three principal divisions:

(a) Medical
(b) Surgical
(c) Laboratory

Such divisions shall be responsible to the Directors of these divisions in the Hospital. All departments of the service shall be grouped under these three heads and each department shall have a Head responsible to the Director of the division to which it belongs.

11. The following shall be responsible to the Medical Director of the Hospital.

(a) The Director of the Medical Service, who shall be responsible for the proper supervision of the work of the Regular Attending Staff on the Medical Wards and in the Medical Division of the Out-patient Department. He shall be a salaried teacher in Medicine in the Bowman Gray School of Medicine. Under him shall be the Resident in Medicine, Medical Interns and other necessary staff.

(b) The Director of the Surgical Service who shall be responsible for the proper supervision of the work of the Regular Attending Staff on the Surgical Wards. He shall be a salaried teacher of Surgery in the Bowman Gray School of Medicine. Under him shall be the Resident in Surgery, Surgical Interns and other necessary staff.

(c) The Director of the Laboratory Service, who shall be responsible for the proper supervision of the work of the Regular Attending Staff in the Department of Pathology, Bacteriology, Serology, Clinical Chemistry, etc., in the Hospital and in the Laboratory Division of the Out-Patient Department. Under him shall be the Resident Pathologist, Pathological Interns and other necessary staff.

12. The organization and grouping of the professional services in the Hospital, the conduct of such services and the assignment of cases shall be under the control of the Medical Director and the Dean of the School of Medicine.

13. All resignations and vacancies occurring in the Regular Attending Staff and in the Resident Medical Staff shall be submitted in writing to the Dean of the Medical School who shall immediately notify the head of the department involved, the Medical Director of the Hospital and the Board of Trustees of the Hospital. Such vacancies shall be filled in accordance with the provisions in Paragraph Five.

14. All resignations from and vacancies occurring in the House Staff (Superintendent of Nurses, Supervisors, Head Nurses, Student Nurses, Dietitians, Orderlies and etc.) shall be made in writing to the Medical Director, who shall immediately notify in writing the Administrator of the Hospital, Dean of the School of Medicine and the Board of Trustees.

Such vacancies shall be filled in accordance with the provisions of Paragraph Five. All vacancies occurring in the Clerical and Maintenance Departments of the Hospital shall be filled by the Administrator of the Hospital.

15. It shall be specifically understood that the School of Medicine shall be financially responsible for its own operation and the North Carolina Baptist Hospital shall be financially responsible for its own maintenance. It is recognized that certain items of expense may be considered to be of joint responsibility. In such cases each shall bear its proportionate share of the cost, which shall be determined by the Administrator of the Hospital and the Dean of the School of Medicine. In case they fail to agree on the proper division of such financial responsibility the matter shall be submitted to the Board of Trustees of the North Carolina Baptist Hospital and the Trustees of Wake Forest College for proper division.

16. It is recognized that a cordial relation between the North Carolina Baptist Hospital and the Bowman Gray School of Medicine will prove of increasing mutual benefit and these relations will be continued, though such relations may be changed if deemed wise by the Board of Trustees of the North Carolina Baptist Hospital, if reasonable notice after conference with the Medical School Authorities is given.

17. The plan provided by this agreement conceives of the North Carolina Baptist Hospital as primarily conducted for the benefit of the sick and needy. To that end every activity of both business and professional staffs must be directed, and every other purpose subordinated. This fundamental idea furnishes a ready means for settling all sincere differences between the administrative and professional branches of the Hospital Service. Cooperation will be promoted by regular conferences which shall be arranged between the Medical Director and the Administrator of the Hospital and the Dean of the School of Medicine. If any differences should arise which cannot be settled in such conferences, then the Medical Director shall report formally to the Dean, and the Hospital Administrator shall report formally to the Board of Trustees for final adjustment.

/s/ *E. L. Davis*

Chairman Board of Trustees, N.C. Baptist Hospital

Signed.

/s/ *Wingate M. Johnson*

Chairman Board of Trustees, Wake Forest College

DATE November 20, 1939

The Memorandum of Understanding Between the North Carolina Baptist Hospital and the Bowman Gray School of Medicine of Wake

Forest College, adopted November 20, 1939, shall be amended. Section 2 on Page 1 shall read as follows:

The Administrator of the Hospital shall be appointed by the Board of Trustees. He shall be directly responsible to the Board of Trustees, of the North Carolina Baptist Hospital. He shall be a member of the faculty of the Bowman Gray School of Medicine of Wake Forest College. He shall be approved and recommended for election by the administration and/or faculty of the Medical School in the same manner as other members of the faculty. The Board of Trustees of the Hospital agrees not to elect an Administrator or other persons to be in charge of the Hospital not so recommended.

Section 3 shall be amended with reference to "a Medical Director" to read "a Medical Director or Chief of Professional Services."

Memorandum of Understanding
Between the
North Carolina Baptist Hospital
and
The Bowman Gray School of Medicine of Wake Forest College

With a view to the promotion of the best medical care, and the best in teaching medical students, interns and para-medical groups, the Board of Trustees of the North Carolina Baptist Hospital and the Trustees of Wake Forest College enter into the following agreement:

1. The practicing physicians in the hospital shall be the faculty members of the Bowman Gray School of Medicine of Wake Forest College.

2. The hospital professional staff chiefs shall meet monthly to consider various professional problems relating to the care of hospital patients and other professional problems of the institution. The organization of the various services within the medical school teaching program shall provide necessary communication for the entire staff (in order to avoid duplication of meetings).

The staff chiefs shall annually elect a Chief of Professional Services who shall work with the Hospital Administrator concerning professional problems. The Chief of Professional Services shall report to the Board of Trustees of the Hospital at its quarterly meetings.

The hospital administrator will meet in an ex officio capacity with the professional staff.

3. It shall be specifically understood that the School of Medicine shall be financially responsible for its own operation and the North Carolina Baptist Hospital shall be financially responsible for its own maintenance. It is recognized that cerain items of expense may be considered to be of joint responsibility. In such cases each shall bear its proportionate share of the cost, which shall be determined by the Administrator of the Hospital and the Dean of the School of Medicine. In case they fail to agree on the proper division of such financial responsibility, the matter

shall be submitted to the Joint Committee of the Board of Trustees of the North Carolina Baptist Hospital and the Trustees of the Wake Forest College for proper division.

4. When it shall become necessary to appoint an Administrator of the Hospital, the Board of Trustees, in recognition of the unique relationship which exists between the Hospital and the Medical School, with the work of each institution being vitally affected by the philosophy and practices of the other, will consult with and seek the approval of the Dean of the Medical School as to the qualifications and fitness of a prospective Administrator of the Hospital before he is appointed; and, when it shall become necessary to appoint a Dean of the Medical School, the Trustees of the College will consult with and seek the approval of the Administrator of the Hospital as to the qualifications and fitness of a prospective Dean before he is appointed. However, it is recognized that the basic and fundamental principles of corporate management require that the Board of Trustees of the Hospital and College have the authority to employ adequate and qualified personnel to carry out and perform all of the duties incident to the corporation's affairs, and to discharge any employee upon his failure to perform adequately the duties assigned.

5. Any differences between the professional and administrative branches which cannot be settled in conference by the Chief of Professional Services, and the Dean of the Medical School and the Hospital Administrator shall be referred to the Joint Committee of Trustees from the Hospital and Wake Forest College for final adjustment.

6/22/58 Passed by Wake Forest College Trustees.

Medical Service Plan

The full-time members of the clinical faculty, operating as the Department of Clinics, devote varying amounts of time, depending on time for teaching, research or administration, to the practice of medicine in service to private patients. The clinic is an official department of the school, and funds are channeled through the regular budget. The school provides space, heat, water, and lights without charge to the clinic; otherwise, the clinic pays all expenses of operation. No claim is made by the school on any part of the income to the physicians in the clinic, but the physicians vote on regular financial support to the school. In two recent expansion programs, the clinic provided over $2 million. The Department of Clinics' present plan of operation follows.

Medical service for private patients by physicians on the full-time faculty is recognized as necessary and desirable for the educational and research programs of the institution, provided that a proper balance between teaching, research, and service is maintained in each participating department. Members of the full-time faculty are eligible to participate in service for private patients if they are licensed by the Board of Medical Examiners of the State of North Carolina and if approved by the dean, the chairman of the department, and the chief of the service concerned. The method of handling fees for medical service is in keeping with the principles approved by the Association of American Medical Colleges and the American Medical Association (1959) as embodied in the following plan:

1. The financial and business affairs of the full-time faculty that relate to the care of private patients is the responsibility of the Department of Clinics of the Bowman Gray School of Medicine. With the approval of the dean, the director of the Department of Clinics, and the chairman of the department concerned, the collection of fees in a specific category may be done through another unit of the medical center. The approval of such an arrangement is based solely on improved efficiency and effectiveness in management.

2. The Department of Clinics is a service department of the medical school. The director is a member of the faculty appointed by and responsible to the dean. A committee of the faculty for the clinic serves in an advisory capacity to the director and the dean.

3. Medical service must be organized under a plan of group endeavor by department or section which is approved by the dean and the chairman and members of the department or section concerned. Such a plan must not impair academic excellence, render an injustice, or threaten the public relations of the institution.

4. The budgets of all departments participating in medical service consist of basic school funds, gifts and grants, and fees for service; all funds are subject to periodic review and annual audit like all other units in the medical school and are incorporated in the financial statement of the medical school each year for the president and Board of Trustees.

5. The individual physician retains the prerogative of establishing fees.

6. The school endorses the "incentive principle." i.e., recognition of variation in individual efficiency in patient care as well as in teaching and research.

7. Institution ceilings are not placed on incomes; time spent in the clinic is limited, and emphasis is placed on the expected and actual

academic contributions of individuals, sections, and departments rather than on income.

8. Full-time faculty are provided offices and examining areas in the medical center without charge and, except for occasional outside consultations, restrict all of their medical service activities to the medical center. In most instances patient examining areas are centralized and separated from the academic space assigned to a department. Charges for clinic services, secretarial assistance, and other unusual and necessary professional expenses are deducted from gross income before it is credited to the department budget. Since 1954 faculty involved in fee for service activity have pledged voluntarily 4 percent of gross income from professional service to the building fund. This was changed to 5 percent of net income in 1966 as a twenty-year pledge to the Medical Center Development Program. In addition, departments and sections have voluntarily established research and development funds, held and administered for them by the medical school through an additional percentage deduction from this income. Together these funds make a significant contribution to the institution.

9. In September, 1962 a new salary plan for all full-time faculty was initiated on a voluntary basis for existing faculty. All new additions to the faculty after this date were required to participate in the plan. In brief, under the plan faculty are salaried under an employer-employee contract with the school. As such, they have guaranteed salaries and become eligible for social security benefits, the insurance program of the school, an elective retirement annuity through Teachers Insurance and Annuity. At this time most of the faculty participate.

James Ralph Scales
President of Wake Forest University since July 1, 1967

Chapter 5

Wake Forest College Moves to Winston-Salem

The Smith Reynolds Foundation Gift

By 1942 appeals for funds had been made on behalf of the medical school to the Smith Reynolds Foundation as well as to all of the large foundations. The first appeal to the foundation was for $21,000 in June, 1941. Will Reynolds, who was president of the foundation, expressed to me his personal approval of the request, but other members of the Board of Directors were more interested in using the income of the foundation in excess of commitments already made to the North Carolina State Board of Health and for the building and development of the Smith Reynolds Airport.

After several conferences with the advisory council and L. D. Long, secretary to Will Reynolds, it was decided that I should visit Mr. Reynolds at his winter home in Orlando, Florida in March 1941 and lay before him the financial needs of the medical school. Mr. Reynolds was quite interested and sympathetic. He took the position, however, that the medical school was secure since it would eventually get more support from the Gray family.

In 1942 I again visited Mr. Reynolds in Orlando. Before that visit a written proposal had been prepared, with the help of the advisory council, for an endowment fund of $10 million to support a program of medical care for the people of northwest North Carolina through the Bowman Gray School of Medicine and the North Carolina Baptist Hospital. Mr. Long, who represented Mr. Reynolds in the major conferences, again advanced the idea that the medical school would get more substantial support through the Gray family. He further suggested that it would be more appropriate for Mr. Reynolds to direct his interest toward strengthening Wake Forest College. I took the position that any support of Wake Forest College would be gratifying to me but that my responsibility was limited to the medical school. Mr. Long suggested that one of the best ways to develop a stronger Wake Forest College would be to move it to Winston-Salem, as had been done in the case of the medical school. On my return to Winston-Salem, I sent the following report of the conference to President Kitchin.

Conference with Mr. W. N. Reynolds and Mr. L. D. Long

Several weeks ago while at the Old Town Club, Mr. L. D. Long, secretary to Mr. W. N. Reynolds for the last twenty years, invited me to visit Orlando, Florida, this winter and play golf with him I told him that I would probably visit Orlando but would not accept his invitation to be his guest while there. About the first of January, I conferred with Mr. Long in his office in the Reynolds Building and explained to him that although Mr. W. N. Reynolds has always expressed a lot of interest in our school and had received me and advised with me freely from time to time, I had never asked him for financial aid. I suggested to Mr. Long that I would like to, if he thought it acceptable to Mr. Reynolds, present the complete picture to him. Mr. Long suggested that I take with me to Orlando all the facts and spend several days at which time we would go over the problem. He suggested that he and I agree on the details before placing the problem before Mr. Reynolds.

I reached Orlando on Wednesday night, January 21, and contacted Mr. Long the next afternoon. We had a very pleasant social afternoon with Mr. Reynolds. The Medical School was not mentioned except casually. The following morning, Mr. Long was occupied with business matters, and in the afternoon we played golf. In the evening of the day, Mr. Long and Mr. Reynolds were occupied with a previously arranged social engagement. The following morning, Mr. Long and Mr. Reynolds, Mrs. Carpenter and I spent a good while at the track taking pictures and seeing Mr. Reynolds' horses. Mrs. Carpenter and Mr. Reynolds continued with the horses and in social intercourse while Mr. Long and I had a long conference on the Medical School. We reviewed carefully an analysis of the situation previously prepared by me. Mr. Long made suggestions for additions tending to put forth more clearly the medical care angle of the plan.

The plan of endowment seemed absolutely good to Mr. Long. The amount requested was never questioned. I was profoundly impressed by the fact that Mr. Reynolds and Mr. Long are very well acquainted with the school, including its needs, and many of the details of its operation. I expressed to Mr. Long my delight in finding this to be true.

Mr. Long further suggested that this analysis not be presented to Mr. Reynolds formally on this visit but that I return to Winston-Salem and mail it to him. The reason for this suggestion was that Mr. Reynolds already has under consideration plans for helping the Medical School and that a direct appeal for funds would be superfluous and might tend to lessen Mr. Reynolds' interest.

At this conference, Mr. Long brought up to me for the second time the question of moving Wake Forest College to Winston-Salem. This he did casually about a year ago. I was informed that within the last few days Mr. Long and Mr. Reynolds had been discussing the possible advantages of such a move. The thought was advanced that it is the desire of Mr. Reynolds that the Bowman Gray School of Medicine be second to none. He has wondered whether it would greatly add to its prestige to be a branch of a much stronger school than Wake Forest College is at the present time. He further advanced the idea that a university in Winston-Salem would tend to decentralize the schools for men, all except Davidson College being located within a short distance of each other in the neighborhood of Raleigh. Mr. Long and Mr. Reynolds have discussed the possibility of Wake Forest College selling its plant at Wake Forest. I offered what appeared to me the best suggestion for a development of this nature, the idea of establishing in Winston-Salem the W. N. Reynolds University, using as its medical school the Bowman Gray School of Medicine and as its undergraduate school of liberal arts Wake Forest College. This is in fact what Duke University did with Trinity College with the exception that they made it the girls' undergraduate school. I further suggested that if such a plan is followed the professional and graduate schools, together with the instruction for juniors and seniors in Winston-Salem, would in fact be an ideal university set up.

The point was not definitely made, but I received the impression that an endowment fund, similar to the one suggested in my outline, and the university idea are now being considered. According to Mr. Long, these two ideas have been discussed by Mr. Reynolds and him since his arrival in Orlando five days prior to my arrival. I was led to believe that they had discussed these matters and that Mr. Reynolds was acquainted with my reasons for being in Orlando.

On Saturday afternoon, Mr. Charles Babcock and Mr. Dick Reynolds flew to Orlando for a conference with Mr. Reynolds relative to some "family project." Mr. Reynolds was occupied with them during the evening and the following morning. Mr. Long and I played golf in the afternoon and were together during the evening with Mrs. Carpenter and Dr. and Mrs. Chappel of Orlando.

Richard J. Reynolds, Jr., left,
and Dr. Harold W. Tribble,
president of Wake Forest College from 1950 to 1967.
Under Dr. Tribble's leadership the college was moved
from the town of Wake Forest to Winston-Salem.

On Sunday, Mr. Reynolds went to Daytona Beach and spent the night visiting Mrs. Reynolds who is there, returning to Orlando Monday morning.

On Monday morning, Mr. Long and I prepared a letter that I am to send Mr. Reynolds on my return to Winston-Salem together with the analysis of the needs of our medical school. At that time, I submitted to Mr. Long certain definite questions that disturbed me concerning the method of approach to Mr. Reynolds for help as follows:

1. In planning charities, is the medical school likely to be left out unless a direct request is made to Mr. Reynolds at this time, the assumption being that if help is wanted, it will be asked for?

Answer: Definitely not. There is no question about Mr. Reynolds' knowledge of your desires, and a direct request at this time would not make help any more likely.

2. In the discussion of the two projects mentioned, an endowment fund and a university, which plans seem uppermost in Mr. Reynolds mind at the present time?

Answer: No opinion.

3. Have you information or an opinion on Dick Reynolds' attitude towards the Grays and the medical school?

Answer: No opinion.

4. Would a direct request to Mr. Reynolds from Mrs. Bernard be received in a friendly manner?

Answer: Most certainly.

5. Would such help?

Answer: No. Not needed.

6. What is Mr. Reynolds' feeling towards the project in consideration of the fact that the school is named for the late Bowman Gray?

Answer: Absolutely good. The late Bowman Gray was Mr. Reynolds' very best friend and he has no feeling of jealousy or envy whatsoever relative to the prominence the project gives his name.

7. If Mr. Reynolds helps the school, would a gift in the near future be more likely or a bequest in his will?

Answer: No opinion. Depends on business conditions.

8. Is there a possibility that Mr. Reynolds may in a substantial amount aid some project outside of Winston-Salem?

Answer: Absolutely not. "Winston-Salem, first, last and always."

9. Has the medical school as good chance as any other big project to obtain help from Mr. Reynolds, and is there any other big project in the way at the present time?

Answer: The medical school has as good chance as any, and there is nothing at the present time in Mr. Reynolds' plans that would prevent his helping the school.

10. If Mr. Reynolds continues to be interested and it appears that a further visit by me would be helpful, can I depend on receiving an invitation to come down again and talk over the plans?

Answer: Most certainly.

Following this conference, Mrs. Carpenter and I went out to the track to tell Mr. Reynolds good-bye.

Impressions

My impressions from this conference and the visit with Mr. Reynolds and Mr. Long are that:

1. They have already discussed from time to time the possibility of helping the medical school. That they had discussed the matter prior to my going to Orlando and that Mr. Reynolds was fully aware of the reason for my visit. My feeling is that that is the reason Mr. Long advised me not to push this point at the present time. In fact, I was told that Mr. Reynolds thinks at the present time that it is his idea and that it would not be a good policy for me to lead him to believe that I had the idea by asking him directly for help.
2. Wake Forest has a possibility of receiving a large grant from Mr. Reynolds.

President Kitchin never replied to my letter.

The Idea Gains Momentum

During the succeeding months Mr. Long and I had several conferences on the matter of moving Wake Forest College to Winston-Salem. Mr. Long was constant in his position that it could be done and that it should be done.

C. J. Jackson, director of the Wake Forest College Expansion Program for $6 million, visited me often in Winston-Salem to discuss the possibility of obtaining funds. He brought a proposal that a $40 million fund be raised to remove the college to Winston-Salem and develop it into a university. He was advised that a similar suggestion had been made to me by Mr. Reynolds and Mr. Long.

A luncheon meeting was arranged by me at the Robert E. Lee Hotel in Winston-Salem on July 16, 1945, with Mr. Long, Mr. Gordon Gray, and Mr. Jackson. That conference began with apparent lack of interest on the part of Mr. Long and Mr. Gray. As a matter of fact, Mr. Long stated later that he tried to avoid the conference but that I "chased him down." As the conference progressed, Mr. Long and Mr. Gray became more interested in going forward. Mr. Gray left the conference and went immediately to see Will Reynolds about the matter. The banner was passed on to Charles H. Babcock, a member of the Board of Directors of the Smith Reynolds Foundation, who, together with Mr. Long and others, brought the proposal to final approval by all parties concerned.

This was not easy. By this time President Kitchin and others, largely from the eastern part of the state, had developed strong opposition to moving the college to Winston-Salem. President Kitchin was so determined to upset the movement he started a new building program on the campus at Wake Forest. He made two significant statements. He said, "I'll sprinkle this campus with buildings and then the college can't be moved." On another occasion, he said to me, "Carpenter, the idea of moving the College to Winston-Salem can never succeed, because I will never agree to it, and they can't move it without the president."

Later he recognized that the move was inevitable, but his loyalty to the old campus made the decision difficult for him to accept.

The Decision to Move the College

The 1945 luncheon conference in Winston-Salem set in motion a chain of events which resulted in Wake Forest College's historic move to a new campus 110 miles across the state. In 1946 the Smith Reynolds Foundation offered Wake Forest $350,000 per year in perpetuity on condition that the College move to Winston-Salem. (The annual payments were increased to $500,000 in 1955 and to $620,000 in 1968.) It was stipulated that the name of the college should not be changed, that its control should continue unaltered and undiminished in the board of trustees chosen by the Baptist State Convention, and that the Baptists of North Carolina, through their convention, should continue at the same level their support of the college.

The Smith Reynolds Foundation proposal was first put in written form in a letter, dated February 27, 1946, from W. N. Reynolds to C. J. Jackson, in which Mr. Reynolds stated, "If this proposal meets with the approval of the College authorities and the requirements set out are met, in my opinion, the Trustees of the Smith Reynolds Foundation would formally approve resolutions carrying out the terms of the proposal."

Charles H. Babcock and his wife, Mary Reynolds Babcock, who were trustees of the Foundation and enthusiastic supporters of the proposal, offered to contribute three hundred acres of the beautiful Reynolda Estate for the new campus.

What happened next is told by Byran Haislip in *A History of the Z. Smith Reynolds Foundation.*

Charles H. Babcock, left,
member of the Board of the Z. Smith Reynolds Foundation,
Coy C. Carpenter, center,
dean of the Bowman Gray School of Medicine,
and C. J. Jackson,
director of development of Wake Forest College, discuss move of the college.

An exchange of correspondence between W. N. Reynolds and Dr. Ralph A. Herring, pastor of the First Baptist Church of Winston-Salem, set the stage for a special meeting of the Board of Trustees of Wake Forest College on March 26, 1946. The trustees created a committee, with former Governor J. M. Broughton as chairman, "to investigate very fully the Reynolds proposal and related matters, such committee to report at a joint meeting of the Board of Trustees of the College and the General Board of the Convention with the Educational Council, to be held at Wake Forest on April 11, 1946." Other members of the committee were Dr. Herring, Judge Johnson J. Hayes, Robert P. Holding, Dr. Thurman Kitchin, Irving E. Carlyle, Dr. Charles H. Durham, and J. Edward Allen.

The public got its first inkling of the matter on the eve of the March 26 meeting of the trustees. Reaction among the state's 600,000 Baptists was dramatic and varied. Many believed it assured the college's future, but others doubted. *Old Gold and Black*, the campus newspaper, recorded the reception of the news in Wake Forest. "An atomic bomb could not have been more sudden, more unexpected, nor stunning," it said.

After the first shock wore off, the offer received closer scrutiny and a rising level of support. Leaders among Baptist laymen in promoting its acceptance included Broughton; Basil M. Watkins, a Durham attorney; Judge Hayes; Mr. Odus M. Mull of Shelby, who was also the leader in obtaining the Bowman Gray fund for the Medical School; and Mr. Carlyle, a Winston-Salem attorney. The college's board of trustees accepted the offer. The General Board of the Baptist State Convention gave its assent, and a full session of the convention was called to meet in Greensboro on July 30, 1946.

Actually, the college's trustees had authority to make the decision. They sought the endorsement of the State Convention as a means of marshaling full support within the denomination for the undertaking.

So, the 3,000 messengers from Baptist churches across the state met and listened to a full day of debate on the proposal. Broughton, as chairman of the special committee, presented the resolution to accept the offer. By a tremendous vote—observers estimated 95 to 97 per cent favored it—the Convention gave approval.

A first, vital question was whether the Foundation legally could commit its income, or a portion of it, to a specific project "in perpetuity." Through a friendly suit, the courts were asked to supply the answer. Chief Justice W. P. Stacy wrote the opinion when the State Supreme Court decided the case. It concluded:

"... finally, after all is said and done the case comes to a relatively narrow compass. Is the contract submitted for judication valid and enforceable? The trial court thought it was. We approve. Wake Forest College has had a long and honorable career and whether it nestles in a forest of Wake, or stands on a knoll in Forsyth, its mission will remain a quest for truth and a crusade for simple right. We have not denied to this great

President Harold W. Tribble
looks over model of new Wake Forest College
in Winston-Salem.

institution and to those whose faith and good works have made it possible this vista of a new dawn and this vision of a new hope."

Following the decision to move the college to Winston-Salem, the Wake Forest campus and other properties in the town of Wake Forest were sold to the Southern Baptist Convention for use of the Southeastern Baptist Theological Seminary which now occupies the campus.

Dr. Kitchin retired as president in 1950, but before his resignation he saw a campaign launched to raise building funds for the new campus. Jens F. Larsen was employed as architect, and a master plan for the campus was adopted.

Dr. Harold W. Tribble, president of Andover Newton Theological Seminary, succeeded Dr. Kitchin in September, 1950, as president of Wake Forest. To Dr. Tribble fell the task of actually moving the college to Winston-Salem and seeing it established in its new home. The new president was a man with immense energy and drive and with great tenacity of purpose. All of these qualities he would need to accomplish the removal. Dr. Tribble plunged immediately into an intensive fund-raising campaign. A challenge gift campaign was begun in the spring of 1951, based upon an anonymous offer of $2 million on condition that the college raise $3 million from other sources. Later the donors were revealed to be W. N. Reynolds, who pledged $1.5 million, and Mrs. Nancy Susan Reynolds of Greenwich, Connecticut who pledged $500,000.

The ground-breaking ceremonies for a new campus were held on October 15, 1951, with President Harry S Truman as the principal speaker. During the ceremonies Mr. Babcock presented Hubert E. Olive, chairman of the Board of Trustees, a deed for the property which would be the college's new home. Actual construction of the college was begun in June, 1952. The first building was Wait Chapel, named in honor of Wake Forest's first president, Samuel Wait. Summer school opened on the new campus on June 18, 1956. The dedication of the campus came on October 18, shortly after the opening of the first fall term.

Until his death on September 10, 1951, W. N. Reynolds continued to guide the Foundation's participation in the removal campaign. In addition, he made personal gifts to the campaign and solicited contributions among his Winston-Salem friends. His interest in the removal campaign also was expressed in his will, which left $1 million to Wake Forest for the construction program and created a trust of

President Harry S. Truman
breaks ground for new Wake Forest College
in Winston-Salem.

approximately $14 million with income payable to the Z. Smith Reynolds Foundation.

The other donor of the $2 million challenge gift, Mrs. Reynolds, has continued to be a loyal friend and patron of Wake Forest. Her latest gift was one of $500,000 that, with a $500,000 gift from the Z. Smith Reynolds Foundation, made possible in 1969 the construction of the Charles H. Babcock School of Business building at Wake Forest. Mrs. Reynolds also gave $1 million for endowment of the Z. Smith Reynolds Library.

Since moving to Winston-Salem, Wake Forest has grown in stature and prestige while continuing to hold fast to the qualities of academic freedom and friendliness for which it has long been known. During its first year in Winston-Salem, the college enrollment, including the professional schools, was 2,185 and 82 percent of the students were from North Carolina.

The enrollment in 1969 was 3,184, and 48 percent were from North Carolina. In 1956–57 the total college budget was a little over $3.5 million. For 1969–70 it was $18,905,116. Scholarships for students totaled $112,185 in 1956–57. Scholarships in 1968–69 totaled $574,000.

Total library volumes have increased from 141,519 to almost 350,000.

These are some of the more obvious changes, and there are many others. Not the least of these is the fact that Wake Forest College became Wake Forest University on June 12, 1967, just before Dr. Tribble and I retired.